ACE YOUR PHYSICAL SCIENCE PROJECT

Titles in the

ACE YOUR PHYSICS SCIENCE PROJECT series:

Ace Your Forces and Motion Science Project: Great Science Fair Ideas

ISBN-13: 978-0-7660-3222-4
ISBN-10: 0-7660-3222-1

Ace Your Math and Measuring Science Project: Great Science Fair Ideas

ISBN-13: 978-0-7660-3224-8
ISBN-10: 0-7660-3224-8

Ace Your Physical Science Project: Great Science Fair Ideas

ISBN-13: 978-0-7660-3225-5
ISBN-10: 0-7660-3225-6

Ace Your Sports Science Project: Great Science Fair Ideas

ISBN-13: 978-0-7660-3229-3
ISBN-10: 0-7660-3229-9

Ace Your Weather Science Project: Great Science Fair Ideas

ISBN-13: 978-0-7660-3223-1
ISBN-10: 0-7660-3223-X

ACE YOUR PHYSICS SCIENCE PROJECT

ACE YOUR PHYSICAL SCIENCE PROJECT

Robert Gardner, Madeline Goodstein, and Thomas R. Rybolt

GREAT SCIENCE FAIR IDEAS

Enslow Publishers, Inc.
40 Industrial Road
Box 398
Berkeley Heights, NJ 07922
USA
http://www.enslow.com

Library of Congress Cataloging-in-Publication Data

Gardner, Robert, 1929–
Ace your physical science project : great science fair ideas / Robert Gardner, Madeline Goodstein, and Thomas R. Rybolt.
p. cm. — (Ace your physics science project)
Includes bibliographical references and index.
Summary: "Presents several science projects and science fair ideas that use physics"—Provided by publisher.
ISBN-13: 978-0-7660-3225-5
ISBN-10: 0-7660-3225-6
1. Physics projects—Juvenile literature. 2. Science projects—Juvenile literature. I. Goodstein, Madeline P. II. Rybolt, Thomas R. III. Title.
QC33.G367 2009
530.078—dc22

2008029637

Printed in the United States of America
102010 Lake Book Manufacturing, Inc., Melrose Park, IL

10 9 8 7 6 5 4 3 2

ISBN-10: 0-7660-3226-4

To Our Readers: We have done our best to make sure all Internet Addresses in this book were active and appropriate when we went to press. However, the author and the publisher have no control over and assume no liability for the material available on those Internet sites or on other Web sites they may link to. Any comments or suggestions can be sent by e-mail to comments@enslow.com or to the address on the back cover.

Enslow Publishers, Inc., is committed to printing our books on recycled paper. The paper in every book contains 10% to 30% post-consumer waste (PCW). The cover board on the outside of each book contains 100% PCW. Our goal is to do our part to help young people and the environment too!

The experiments in this book are a collection of the authors' best experiments, which were previously published by Enslow Publishers, Inc., in *Fish Tank Physics Projects*, *Science Project Ideas About Air*, *Science Project Ideas About Kitchen Chemistry*, *Science Projects About Kitchen Chemistry*, *Science Projects About Solids, Liquids, and Gases*, and *Soda Pop Science Projects: Experiments with Carbonated Soft Drinks*.

Illustration Credits: Enslow Publishers, Inc., Figures 2–6, 8, 19, 22, 23, 25; Jacob Katari, Figures 16–18; Stephen Delisle, Figures 1, 7, 9–15, 20, 21, 24, 26–28; Tom LaBaff, Figure 29.

Photo Credits: NASA, p. 12; Shutterstock, p. 36

Cover Photos: Shutterstock

CONTENTS

● ***Indicates experiments that offer ideas for science fair projects.***

CHAPTER 4

The Properties of Gases 71

CHAPTER 5

Physical and Chemical Changes 91

● ***Indicates experiments that offer ideas for science fair projects.***

INTRODUCTION

When you hear the word *science*, do you think of a person in a white lab coat surrounded by beakers of bubbling liquids, specialized lab equipment, and computers? What exactly is science? Maybe you think science is only a subject you learn in school. Science is much more than this.

Science is the study of the things that are all around you, every day. No matter where you are or what you are doing, scientific principles are at work. You don't need special materials or equipment, or even a white lab coat, to be a scientist. Materials commonly found in your home, at school, or at a local store will allow you to become a scientist and pursue an area of interest. By making careful observations and asking questions about how things work, you can begin to design experiments to investigate a variety of questions. You can do science. You probably already have but just didn't know it!

Perhaps you are reading this book because you are looking for an idea for a science fair project for school, or maybe you are just hoping to find something fun to do on a rainy day. This book will provide an opportunity to conduct experiments and collect data to learn more about physical science. You will learn about the different states of matter and the properties of solids, liquids, and gases. You will likely gain a better understanding of the properties of matter and have fun along the way!

SCIENCE FAIR PROJECT IDEAS

Many of the experiments in this book may be appropriate for science fair projects. Experiments marked with a symbol (🏆) include a section called Science Fair Project Ideas. The ideas in this section will provide suggestions to help you develop your own original science fair project. However, judges at such fairs do not reward projects or experiments that are simply copied from a book. For example, a model of a molecule, commonly found at these fairs, would probably not impress judges unless it was done in a novel way. On the other hand, a carefully performed experiment to find out how temperature affects the solubility of different substances would be likely to receive careful consideration.

THE SCIENTIFIC METHOD

All scientists look at the world and try to understand how things work. They make careful observations and conduct research about a question. Different areas of science use different approaches. Depending on the phenomenon being investigated, one method is likely to be more appropriate than another. Designing a new medication for heart disease, studying the spread of an invasive plant species such as purple loosestrife, and finding evidence about whether there was once water on Mars all require different methods.

Despite the differences, however, all scientists use a similar general approach to do experiments. It is called the scientific method. In most experiments, some or all of the following steps are used: making an observation, formulating a question, making a hypothesis (an answer to the question) and prediction (an if-then statement), designing and conducting an experiment, analyzing results and drawing conclusions, and accepting or rejecting the hypothesis. Scientists then share their findings with others by writing articles that are published in journals. After—and only after—a hypothesis has repeatedly been supported by experiments it can be considered a theory.

You might be wondering how to get an experiment started. When you observe something in the world, you may become curious and think of a question. Your question can be answered by a well-designed investigation. Your question may also arise from an earlier experiment or from background reading. Once you have a question, you should make a hypothesis. Your hypothesis is a possible answer to the question (what you think will happen). Once you have a hypothesis, it is time to design an experiment.

In most cases, it is appropriate to do a controlled experiment. This means that there are two groups treated exactly the same except for the single factor that you are testing. That factor is often called a variable. For example, if you want to investigate whether temperature affects the solubility of salt in water, two groups may be used. One group is called the control group, and the other is called the experimental group. The two groups should be treated exactly the same: The same type of container should be used in each, the containers should contain the same volume of water, the water should be stirred the same number of times, and so forth. The control group will be the beaker kept in a pan maintained at room temperature while the experimental group will be the beaker kept in a pan maintained at a higher temperature. The variable is temperature—it is the thing that changes, and it is the only difference between the two groups.

During the experiment, you will collect data. In this example, you might measure the amount of salt (in grams) that dissolves in the water in each beaker. By comparing the data collected from the control group with the data collected from the experimental group, you will draw conclusions. Since the two groups are treated exactly alike except for temperature, an increased number of grams of salt dissolving in the beaker of water maintained at a higher temperature would allow you to conclude with confidence that increased solubility is a result of the one thing that was different: higher temperature.

Two other terms that are often used in scientific experiments are *dependent* and *independent* variables. The dependent variable here is the amount of salt that dissolves, because solubility depends upon temperature. Temperature is the independent variable (it doesn't depend on anything). After the data is collected, it is analyzed to see whether the hypothesis was supported or rejected. Often, the results of one experiment will lead you to a related question, or they may send you off in a different direction. Whatever the result, there is something to be learned from all scientific experiments.

SCIENCE FAIRS

Science fair judges tend to reward creative thought and imagination. However, it's difficult to be creative or imaginative unless you are really interested in your project. Take the time to choose a topic that really appeals to you. Consider, too, your own ability and the cost of materials. Don't pursue a project that you can't afford.

If you decide to use a project found in this book for a science fair, you will need to find ways to modify or extend it. This should not be difficult because you will probably find that as you do these projects new ideas for experiments will come to mind. These new experiments could make excellent science fair projects, particularly because they spring from your own mind and are interesting to you.

If you decide to enter a science fair and have never done so before, you should read some of the books listed in the Further Reading section. The books that deal specifically with science fairs will provide plenty of helpful hints and lots of useful information that will enable you to avoid the pitfalls that sometimes plague first-time entrants. You will learn how to prepare appealing reports that include charts and graphs, how to set up and display your work, how to present your project, and how to relate to judges and visitors.

SAFETY FIRST

As with many activities, safety is important in science, and certain rules apply when conducting experiments. Some of the rules below may seem obvious to you, but each is important to follow.

1. Have **an adult** help you whenever the book advises.
2. Wear eye protection and closed-toe shoes (rather than sandals), and tie back long hair.
3. Don't eat or drink while doing experiments, and never taste substances being used.
4. Avoid touching chemicals.
5. Keep flammable substances away from fire.

6. When doing these experiments, use only nonmercury thermometers, such as those filled with alcohol. The liquid in some thermometers is mercury. It is dangerous to breathe mercury vapor. If you have mercury thermometers, **ask an adult** to take them to a local mercury thermometer exchange location.
7. Do only those experiments that are described in the book or those that have been approved by **an adult**.
8. Never engage in horseplay or play practical jokes.
9. Before beginning, read through the entire experimental procedure to make sure you understand all the instructions, and clear all extra items from your work space.
10. At the end of every activity, clean all materials and put them away. Wash your hands thoroughly with soap and water.

On the Moon, an astronaut weighs less, but has the same mass as on Earth.

Matter: Gases, Liquids, and Solids

MATTER IS ANYTHING THAT HAS MASS AND TAKES UP SPACE. This book is matter, your body is matter, the water you drink is matter, and the air you breathe is matter. Matter exists in one of three states: solid, liquid, or gas.

Mass is a measure of the amount of matter. Mass can usually be found with a balance or scale. There is a difference between mass and weight. Mass is the amount of matter in an object. It is the same everywhere. If your mass is 50 kilograms (kg), it will be 50 kg on the moon or anywhere else. Your weight is the force with which gravity pulls on you. Newtons are the units used to measure force. If your mass is 50 kg, you will weigh nearly 500 newtons (N) (110 pounds) on Earth. Any mass of 50 kg will weigh nearly 500 N on Earth. On the moon, where gravity is weaker, you would weigh only about 80 N (18 pounds), but your mass would still be 50 kg. There is no less of you on the moon than on Earth, but the Moon does not pull as hard on you as Earth does.

Since all the experiments in this book are to be done on Earth, the difference between mass and weight will not usually be important. Consequently, mass units will be used throughout. Occasionally, when gravity plays a role, we will use the term *weight* instead of mass.

We will express the force of gravity in units of grams-weight (g-wt) or kilograms-weight (kg-wt) so you will not have to deal with newtons. Newtons are probably less familiar to you than grams or kilograms.

The amount of space a chunk of matter occupies is known as its volume. Volume can be found in a number of different ways, as you shall see.

1.1 The States of Matter

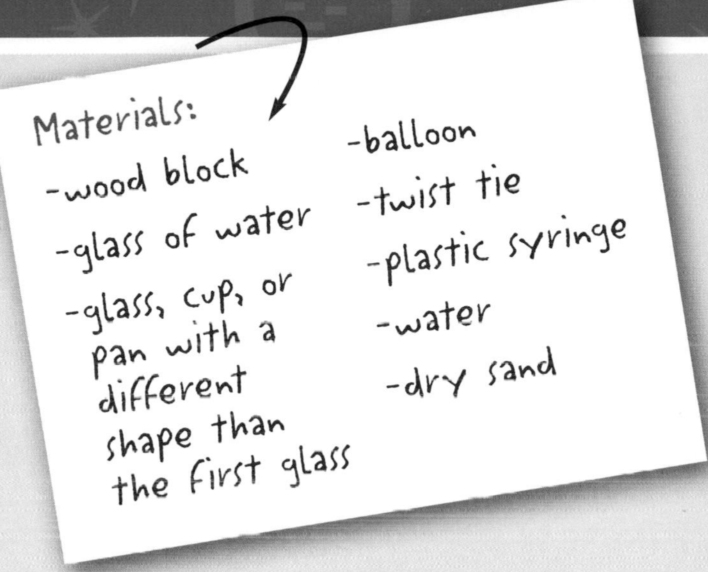

Matter comes in three states: solid, liquid, or gas. Most of the things we handle in our daily lives are solids, but nearly three-fourths of the planet we live on is covered by liquid—water! Above Earth's land and seas is an invisible blanket of gas more than 100 kilometers (60 miles) thick. This gas is the air that makes up Earth's atmosphere. Air is actually a mixture of gases, mostly nitrogen (78 percent) and oxygen (21 percent).

A block of wood can serve as a typical solid. Does it have a definite shape? Does it have a fixed (unchanging) volume? As long as no force acts on the solid, does either its shape or volume change?

Water is a liquid. Pour some water into a glass, cup, or pan. Then pour it into a container with a different shape. Does a liquid have a definite shape? Or does it take the shape of the container it is in? As long as none of the water is allowed to evaporate, is its volume fixed?

Air can serve as a typical gas. Blow some air into a balloon and seal its neck with a twist tie. Can you change the shape of the gas in the balloon? Does a gas have a fixed shape? Or does it take the shape of the container it is in? Now remove the twist tie so the air can escape. Does a gas have a fixed volume? Where is the gas that left the balloon?

Another way to examine some properties of a gas is with an empty plastic syringe. As shown in Figure 1a, lift up the plunger to draw some air into the syringe. Place your finger over the end of the syringe and push the plunger farther into the cylinder as shown in Figure 1b. Did you change the shape of the gas? Did you change its volume? What happens if you keep your finger tightly against the open end of the syringe and release the plunger?

Were you able to compress a gas—that is, squeeze it into a smaller volume? Try the same thing with water. Draw about half a cylinderful of

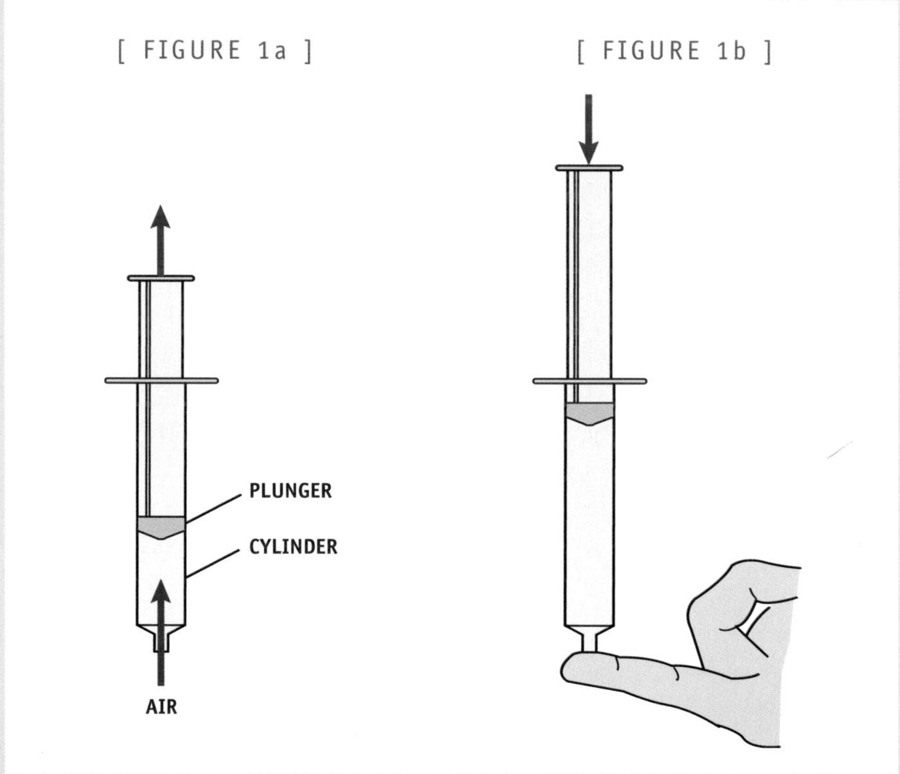

1a) Pull the plunger of a syringe outward to draw air into the cylinder. b) Put your finger firmly over the open end of the syringe and push the plunger inward. Can you squeeze air into a much smaller volume?

water into the syringe. Place your finger tightly against the open end of the cylinder and try to push the plunger inward. Can you compress a liquid?

Do you think you can compress something that seems solid? To find out, fill the cylinder of a plastic syringe with dry sand. Place your finger over the open end, then try to push the plunger down. Can you compress a solid?

AN ATOMIC MODEL OF MATTER

To explain the different states of matter and other chemical properties, an English chemist named John Dalton developed an atomic model of matter early in the nineteenth century. According to his atomic theory, elements are the basic substances in matter. They consist of identical particles called atoms. Hydrogen, oxygen, iron, aluminum, carbon, and so on are elements. The atoms of any one element are identical, but the atoms of different elements differ in mass. Oxygen atoms, for example, are 16 times more massive than hydrogen atoms, 4/3 more massive than carbon atoms, but only 1/2 as massive as sulfur atoms.

Compounds are substances formed by the chemical joining of two or more elements. The atoms of different elements sometimes combine, always in a fixed ratio, to form molecules. Molecules are the fundamental particles that make up compounds. For example, two atoms of hydrogen combine with one atom of oxygen to form a molecule of water.

In a gas, the atoms or molecules are far apart, in constant motion, and free to move virtually independently of one another. Because the particles of a gas are so far apart, a certain volume of gas has far less mass than the same volume of a liquid or solid. The large distance between gas molecules makes it possible to compress a gas—squeeze it into a much smaller volume. And because gas molecules are in constant motion, they will fill any enclosed space in which they are placed.

In a liquid, the molecules or atoms are touching but are free to move around one another. Because the molecules of a liquid are close together, a liquid cannot be compressed. However, the molecules can slide around one another and, therefore, can take the shape of any vessel into which they are poured.

Solids are of a fixed shape and volume because, as with liquids, their atoms or molecules are touching one another. Unlike liquids, the molecules of a solid are not free to move about one another. They are in fixed positions and can only vibrate in place. Since the fundamental particles of a solid are in fixed positions, the shape of a solid remains the same regardless of where it is placed.

Experimental evidence shows that the speed at which atoms and molecules move is related to their temperature. When heat is added to matter, the average speed of the molecules that make up that matter increases. Even the atoms or molecules in solids vibrate more rapidly as their temperature rises. In fact, the kinetic energy of molecules—the energy associated with their motion—can be shown to be in proportion to temperature.

1.2 Measuring the Volume of Matter

Materials:
- scissors
- ruler
- pencil
- light cardboard
- modeling clay
- graduated cylinder
- olive jar
- marking pen
- masking tape
- stone that will fit in the graduated cylinder
- water
- dishpan
- sink
- a partner
- balloon

Using scissors, a ruler, and a pencil, cut a square 1.0 centimeter (cm) on a side from a piece of light cardboard. The upper surface of the square has an area that is defined as 1.0 square centimeter (cm^2). The area of a square or rectangle is length times width, and $1.0 \text{ cm} \times 1.0 \text{ cm} = 1.0 \text{ cm}^2$. Now pull the square over a distance of 1.0 cm, as shown in Figure 2, to sweep out a

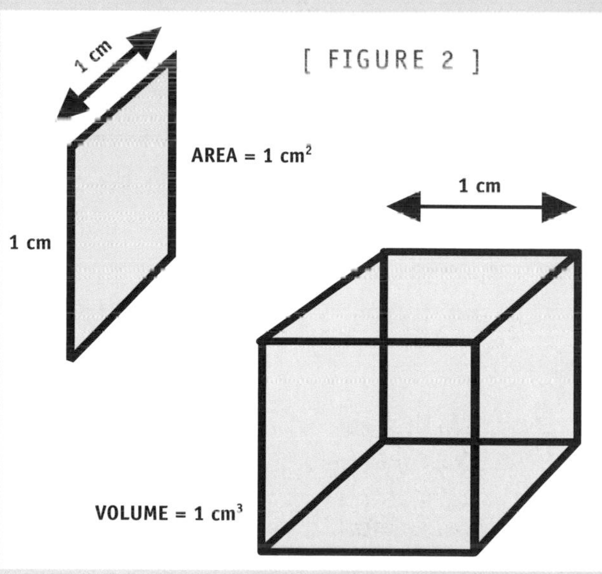

[FIGURE 2]

Drag a square 1.0 cm on a side through a distance of 1.0 cm. You will have swept out a volume of 1.0 cubic centimeter.

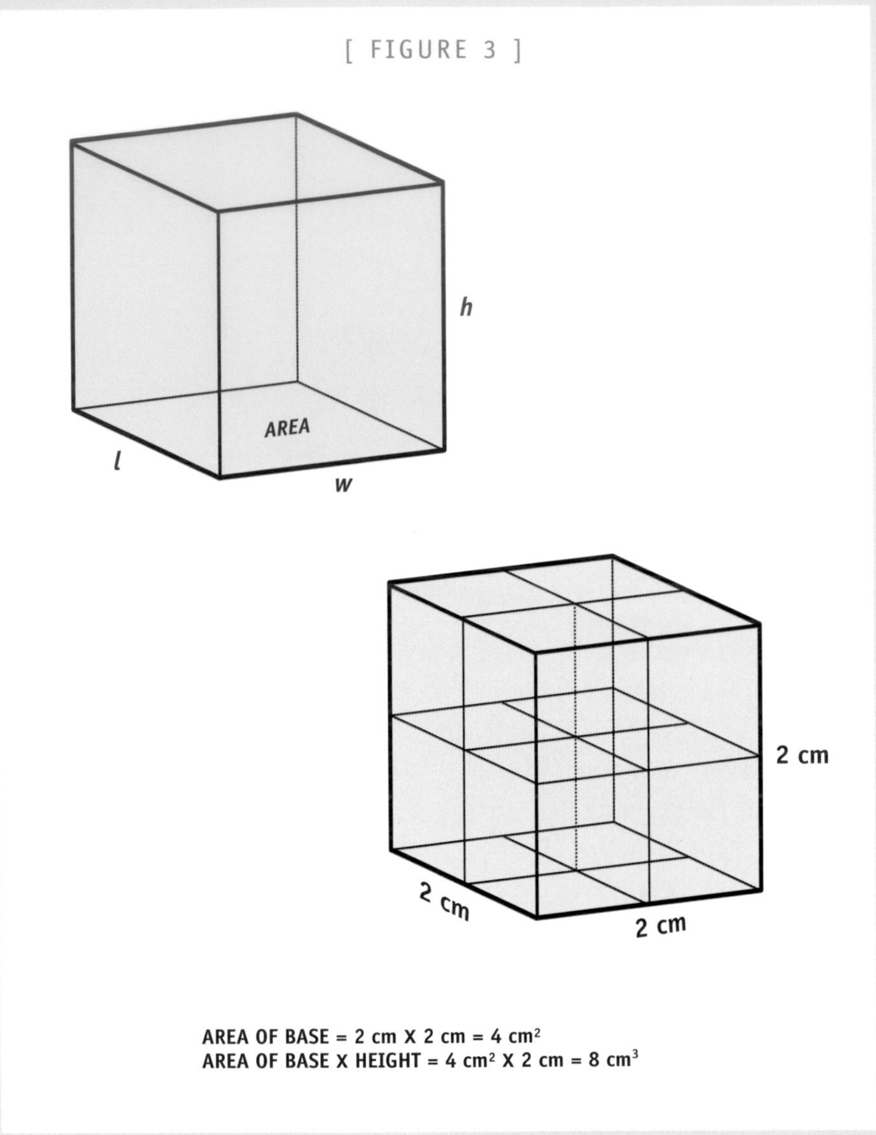

The volume (V) of any regular solid is equal to the area of the base ($l \times w$) times the height (h); consequently, V = lwh. As an example: 2 cm × 2 cm × 2 cm = 8 cm^3. Notice that each layer contains 4 cubic centimeters. There are two layers for a total of 8 cm^3.

volume. The volume swept out by the square is 1.0 cm^3 (cubic centimeter). The volume of a regular solid is equal to the area of its base times its height, and 1.0 cm^2 × 1.0 cm = 1.0 cm^3.

The volume you swept out was a cube, because its length, width, and height were all equal. Use some clay to make a solid cube that is 1.0 cm in length, width, and height. What is the volume of the cube? Show that the total surface area of all the sides of the cube is 6.0 cm^2.

As shown in Figure 3, the volume of any regular solid is given by the formula:

Volume = area of base (length × width) × height, or $V = lwh$.

In order to find the volume of matter in a cylinder, you will need to use a formula that includes π (pi), which is the ratio of a circle's circumference to its diameter. Its value is approximately 3.14. The volume of a cylinder (see Figure 4) is $\pi r^2 h$, where r is the radius of the base of the cylinder, h is its height, and π is approximately 3.14. The number you attach to a volume depends on the units used to measure the radius and the height. You could use inches just as well as centimeters, or yards as well as meters. In this book, we will use metric units (millimeters, centimeters, meters, etc.) throughout because the metric system is used for most scientific measurements.

[FIGURE 4]

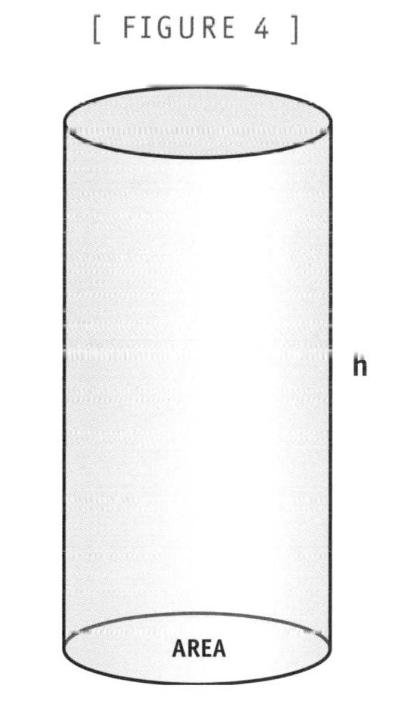

The volume of a cylinder is equal to $\pi r^2 h$.

The volume of regular solids, such as cubes, cylinders, and rectangular solids (parallelepipeds), can be found by multiplying the area of the

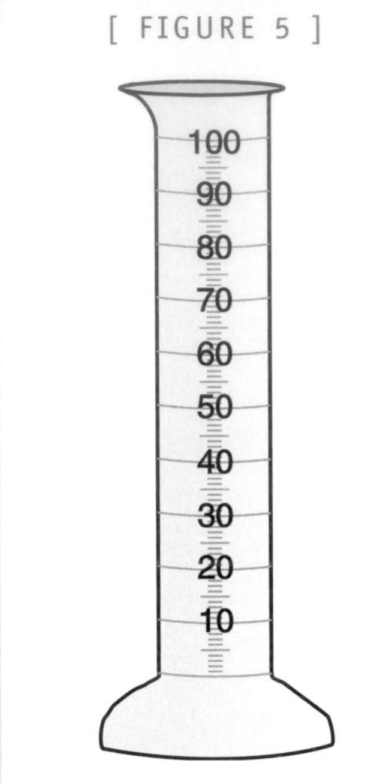

The cylinder shown here is graduated into intervals of 1.0 cm^3 or 1.0 ml.

base by the height. But how can you find the volume of a solid with an irregular shape such as a stone?

To understand how the volume of a stone can be measured, you need to first see how the volume of a liquid can be measured. As you saw in Experiment 1.1, a liquid has no fixed shape. It takes the shape of the vessel into which it is poured. We can use this property of liquids to determine their volumes. Usually, this is done by pouring the liquid into a hollow cylinder called a graduated cylinder. A graduated cylinder, like the one in Figure 5, has horizontal lines along its side that are used to measure the volume of its contents.

Suppose the cylinder has a diameter of 3.57 cm. Its radius (1.785 cm), when squared and multiplied by π, is 10.0 cm^2. If the horizontal lines on the side of such a graduated cylinder are spaced 1.0 cm apart, the space between lines is 10 cm^3, because 10.0 $cm^2 \times 1.0$ cm = 10 cm^3.

You may find that a commercially-made graduated cylinder is marked in milliliters (ml). A milliliter, as its name indicates, is 1/1,000 of a liter (l). It has the same volume as a cubic centimeter (1 cm^3 = 1 ml). Therefore, 1,000 ml and 1,000 cm^3 both equal 1.0 liter.

Make a graduated cylinder using a tall glass cylinder, such as a jar that olives come in. To prevent the lines from being rubbed off, attach a vertical strip of masking tape to the side of the jar and make the marks on the tape. Mark a zero (0) line at the bottom of the tape. Carefully measure the diameter and calculate the cross-sectional area of the jar. Then use a marking pen and ruler to make lines that correspond to 10 ml intervals above the 0 line.

When you have finished making your graduated cylinder, you can check it in a school lab. Pour known volumes of water from a graduated cylinder or metric measuring cup into the graduated cylinder you made. Be sure you use the bottom of the curved meniscus (see Figure 6) to measure the volume. Water adheres to glass or plastic so that a thin ring of water in contact with the glass rises higher than the rest of the water. The actual volume of the water is below the bottom of the meniscus.

How closely does the volume measured in the commercial graduated cylinder agree with the volume as measured in your homemade one?

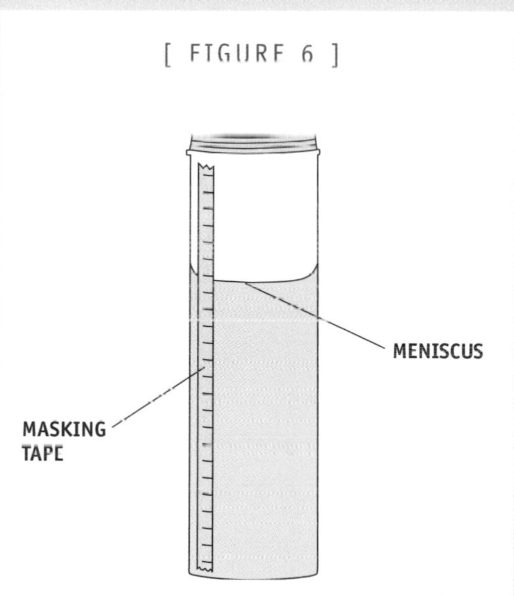

The volume of a liquid should be measured from the bottom of the meniscus.

You can now find the volume of a solid with an irregular shape, such as a stone. Two different pieces of matter cannot occupy the same space. With a graduated cylinder, you can measure the volume of an irregular solid. Note the exact volume of some water in a graduated cylinder. Then carefully lower the stone into the cylinder. What happens to the water level? How much water did the stone displace? What is the volume of the stone?

The volume of many gases can be measured in the same way. To do this, get a partner to join you. You will need a balloon. Add several inches of water to a dishpan in a sink. Then fill a graduated cylinder with water, cover the top of the cylinder with a cardboard square, hold the square firmly against the cylinder as you invert it and place it in the pan of water, as shown in Figure 7a. Have your partner hold the cylinder in place while you put the neck of an inflated balloon under the mouth of the graduated cylinder in the dishpan. Partially release the neck of an inflated balloon so that bubbles of air rise up the graduated cylinder (see Figure 7b). As you can see, the gas replaces the water in the cylinder. How much air was in the balloon? How could you measure the volume of a large volume of gas, a volume larger than the volume of the graduated cylinder?

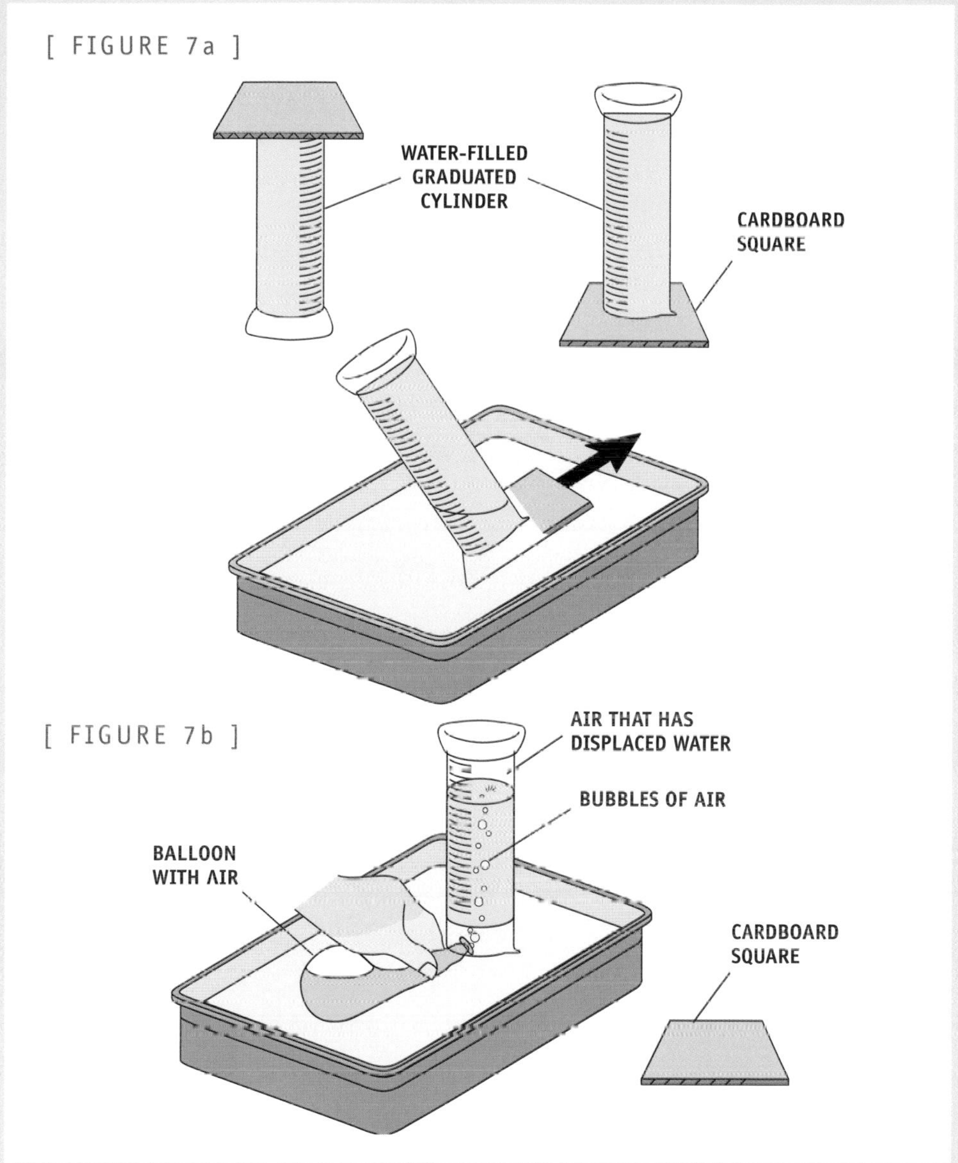

7a) Cover the mouth of a graduated cylinder with a cardboard square. Then invert the cylinder and place its covered mouth under water. b) Allow gas from a balloon to displace water from the graduated cylinder.

Science Fair Project Ideas

- Design an experiment to measure the volume of air that you normally inhale and exhale during breathing. Then find the largest amount of air that you can exhale after taking a deep breath.
- How would you measure the volume of a gas that dissolves in water?
- Show that the surface area of a cylinder is $2\pi r^2 + 2\pi rh$.
- Show that the volume of a cone is $1/3\ \pi r^2 h$, where r is the radius of the cone's circular base and h is the vertical height of the cone.
- Demonstrate that the volume of a sphere is $4/3\ \pi r^3$, where r is the radius of the sphere.

1.3 Measuring the Mass in Matter

Materials:
- an adult
- wooden meterstick or yardstick
- string
- drill and bits
- ruler
- finishing nail
- 2 large cans
- sand
- bench or small table
- 2 large paper clips
- string
- aluminum pie pans
- modeling clay
- small paper clips or washers
- two 30-mL plastic medicine cups
- calibrated eyedropper or graduated cylinder

If you have a balance or scale, you can use it to measure mass. If not, you can make one from a meterstick or yardstick, aluminum pie pans, string, a nail, and paper clips.

Ask an adult to drill three small holes through a wooden meterstick, as shown in Figure 8a. The hole at the 18-inch mark should be slightly above the center of the yardstick. A hole one inch from each end of the balance should be 0.25 inch above the lower side of the meterstick. Slide a finishing nail snugly through the middle hole to serve as a pivot point for the balance beam (yardstick). Opposite ends of the pivot nail can rest on two large sand-filled cans set on a bench or small table.

Next, open two large paper clips. Slip the wider end of each paper clip through the holes at the ends of the balance beam. **Ask an adult** to drill three small holes in each of the pie pans, as shown in Figure 8b. String

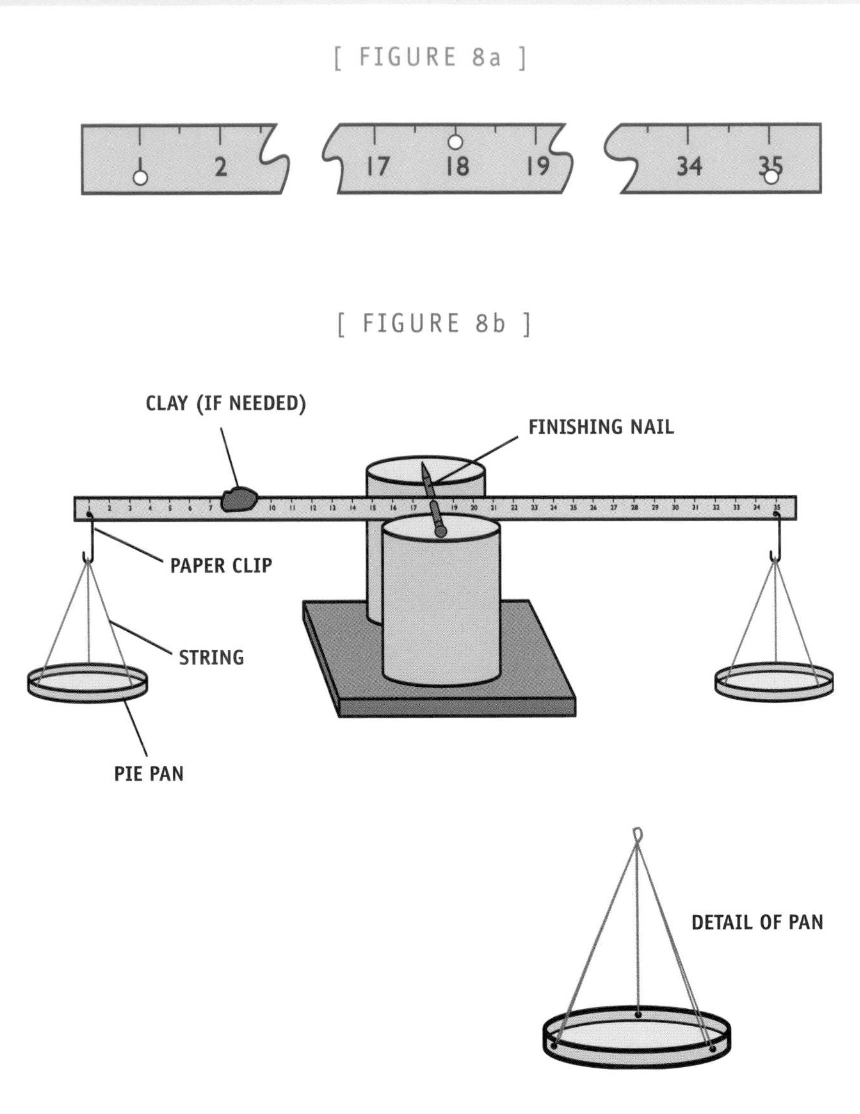

8a) Drill three holes through a wooden yardstick, as shown. A nail through the center hole can serve as a pivot for the balance beam. b) Add pans, and you have made a sensitive balance.

can be used, as shown, to hang small pie tins from the paper clips at each end of the beam. If the balance beam is not level after the pans are in place, add a small piece of clay to the lighter (turned-up) side. Move the clay along the top of the balance beam until it is level.

You can now use the balance to weigh a variety of small objects by seeing how much mass you must place in the right-hand pan to balance the object in the left-hand pan.

Since you probably do not have a standard set of gram masses, you can use identical paper clips or small washers as your unit of mass. To convert these masses to grams, you will have to find out how many paper clips or washers equal one gram. You can do this by placing identical, empty 30-ml plastic medicine cups on opposite pans of the balance. If the beam is not level, move the clay until it is level. Use a calibrated eyedropper or graduated cylinder to add exactly 20 ml of water to the medicine cup on the left-hand pan.

The mass of 20 ml of water is 20 grams (g). To determine the mass of a single paper clip or washer, add these small masses to the right-hand pan of your balance until they balance the 20 g of water on the other pan. It will probably require about 40 paper clips to balance 20 g of water. The number of washers will depend on their size.

If the last paper clip or washer you add tips the balance beyond its level position, place that paper clip on the beam, as you did the clay, and move it until balance is achieved. How can you use that paper clip to make an accurate measurement of the mass of the water to the nearest fraction of a paper clip unit? Whatever your measurement in paper clips, it is equal to 20 g. How can you use the information you have just obtained to find the mass of one paper clip in grams?

Use your balance to weigh a number of different solids and liquids. What is the smallest mass your balance can measure? Can you measure the mass of a drop of water? If not, can you measure the mass of ten drops? Of 100 drops? How can you use the mass of 100 drops to find the mass of one drop?

Science Fair Project Ideas

- In building your balance, you were told to make the center hole at the 18-inch mark *above* the center of the balance beam. The pans were hung 0.25 inch above the *bottom* of the beam. To explore the effect of the position of the center and end holes on a balance, you can use a piece of pegboard about 17 inches long by 2 inches wide with small holes about 1/2 inch apart. The pegboard balance beam should be a little more than three holes wide and 35 holes long. It can be suspended from a nail driven into a post or upright board. Large paper clips can be used to suspend the pans from the ends of the beam. Vary the positions of the center pivot and the suspension positions of the pans. How and why do the positions of the pivot point and pan suspensions affect the balance?
- See if you can build a balance that will measure very small masses such as a postage stamp. Then see if you can build a balance that will measure large masses such as you and your friends.
- One of the fundamental laws of nature is the law of conservation of mass, which states that mass cannot be created or destroyed. **Under adult supervision**, design and carry out experiments to show that mass is conserved during chemical reactions as well as during physical changes such as melting and freezing.

1.4 Finding the Density of Liquids and Solids

Materials:

- an adult if you use liquids other than those listed
- balance you made in Experiment 1.3 or suitable substitute
- metric ruler
- block of wood, lump of modeling clay, and other solids such as steel washers and pieces of metal such as copper, brass, aluminum, or coins
- different kinds of wood (pine, balsa, maple, or oak)
- pen or pencil
- notebook
- graduated cylinder or metric measuring cup
- liquids: water, rubbing alcohol, vinegar, fruit juices, milk, Gatorade, molasses, baby oil, and cooking oil

The ability to measure volume and mass provides you with a way to determine a characteristic property that can be used to help identify substances. That property is density—a measure of the compactness of matter. It tells you how much matter is packed into a certain volume. Density is defined as mass divided by volume.

To find the density of a substance, you need to weigh a known volume of that substance. For example, you might find that a piece of cork with a volume of 100 cm^3 weighs 25 g. You would calculate its density to be 0.25 g/cm^3 because

$$\frac{25\ \text{g}}{100\ \text{cm}^3} = 0.25\ \text{g/cm}^3.$$

To obtain the information needed to determine the density of a solid with a regular shape, you can simply measure its dimensions with a ruler, calculate its volume, and then weigh it. How would you find the density of a solid with an irregular shape, such as a lump of clay?

To find the density of a liquid, you can weigh an empty graduated cylinder or metric measuring cup. Then add a known volume of liquid to the cylinder or cup and weigh again. How can you use these measurements to find the density of the liquid?

One liquid whose density is very useful for scientific purposes is water. Water is used as a standard for many other measurements such as mass, heat, temperature, solubility, acidity, and density.

Design an experiment to determine the density of water. Take into consideration the accuracy of your balance and graduated cylinder or measuring cup when deciding what volume to use. For example, if you can measure volume to only the nearest milliliter, you certainly want to use more than 10 ml of water. An error of 1 ml in 10 ml means you can only measure to $\pm$ 10 percent (1 part in 10 parts). Generally, you want to weigh as large a volume as is practical so that you can be as accurate as possible. For example, an error of 1 ml in 100 ml enables you to measure volume to within 1 percent. The same is true of mass; the larger the mass, the less the error. Of course, you have to take into account the limitations of the available instruments. A large graduated cylinder may not fit on your balance, and a balance is limited by the mass it can accommodate.

Generally, 100 cm^3 of a liquid or solid will provide sufficient accuracy. With a balance that can measure to 1/10 of a gram, 10 ml will be sufficient if the volume can be measured to 1/10 of a cubic centimeter.

Taking the accuracy of your measuring tools into account, determine the density of a block of wood, a lump of clay, and a variety of other solids. Steel washers, pieces of copper, brass, aluminum, and other metals such as coins may be available. You can also use different kinds of wood (pine, balsa, maple, or oak). As you work, record your measurements and calculations in a notebook.

Which solid was the densest? Which was the least dense? Of the woods you measured, which was the most dense? Which was the least dense?

Now turn your attention to liquids. Remember to measure their volume using the bottom of the meniscus. After confirming that the density of water is 1.0 g/cm^3, you might measure the masses of known volumes of a number of other liquids that may be available. Rubbing alcohol, vinegar, fruit juices, milk, Gatorade, molasses, baby oil, and cooking oil are good choices. **Check with an adult** before trying other liquids. Again, record your measurements and calculations in a notebook.

Science Fair Project Ideas

- The density of isopropyl alcohol (isopropanol) is 0.79 g/cm^3. Isopropanol is the main ingredient in rubbing alcohol. What did you find the density of rubbing alcohol to be? Examine the label on the bottle of rubbing alcohol you used. What fraction of the liquid is isopropanol? Assuming the other ingredient is water, what would you expect the density of rubbing alcohol to be? How does that value compare with the density you calculated from your measurements? How might you explain any differences between the density expected and the density calculated?
- Before a standard metal kilogram weight was established, a liter of water served as a suitable substitute. Show that the mass of 1.0 liter of water is 1.0 kg.
- Investigate how water is used as a standard for other measurements such as heat, temperature, solubility, acidity, and density.
- Does the amount of matter affect a substance's density? That is, would the density of 100 ml of water be different from the density of 200 ml?

1.5 Density and Floating

Materials:
- lump of clay that weighs about 50 grams
- balance you built in Experiment 1.3 or another balance or scale
- water
- metric measuring cup

Do you think the density of a solid can be used to determine whether it will sink or float in water?

To find out, use what you learned in the previous experiment in which you measured the densities of a number of different solids. Take those solids that are more dense than water and place them in water. Do they sink or float? Then take those solids that are less dense than water and place them in water. Do they sink or float? What can you conclude?

What about steel ships? You probably found that steel is more dense than water. Nevertheless, steel ships float in water. Perhaps you can understand why they float by doing another experiment.

Prepare a lump of clay that weighs about 50 grams. You can weigh the clay on the balance you built in Experiment 1.3 or on another balance or scale. Next, add about 200 ml of water to a metric measuring cup. Place the lump of clay in the measuring cup. How much water does the clay displace? What is the volume of the clay?

According to the measurements you have made, what is the density of the clay? Does the density of clay that you just determined agree with the density you calculated for clay in the previous experiment?

Now reshape the lump of clay. Mold it into a dish-shaped vessel with high sides. Note the water level in the metric measuring cup. Then carefully lower the clay onto the water in that cup. If the clay does not float, remove it and mold it some more until it will float. Once the clay floats, note the water level in the cup. How much water does the clay displace now? How many grams would that volume of water weigh? How does the weight of the water displaced compare with the weight of the clay?

Using what you have learned, see if you can explain why steel boats can float.

The Properties of Liquids

IN THIS CHAPTER, YOU WILL LEARN ABOUT THE PROPERTIES OF LIQUIDS. Liquids have properties that make them different from solids and gases. For example, the atoms in a liquid are not as tightly packed as in solids and do not maintain their shape. What happens when a solid is added to a liquid? Have you ever watched colored, flavored crystals disappear in water as you stirred them while preparing a cool drink on a hot day? When a solid, such as sugar, disappears in a liquid, we say the solid, or *solute*, has dissolved in the liquid, or *solvent*, to make a *solution*.

Since sugar is soluble in water, does that mean it is soluble in other liquids such as alcohol? Does solubility—the amount of solute that dissolves in a fixed amount of solvent—depend on the solute? Does temperature affect the amount of solute that can dissolve in water? How do solvents other than water behave? Will liquids dissolve in other liquids? What is viscosity? You can find the answers to these questions and many more by doing the experiments in this chapter.

2.1 Experimenting With Solutions

Materials:
- sugar
- measuring teaspoon
- spoon
- 2 drinking glasses
- water
- measuring cup
- card or ruler
- cold water
- hot water
- kosher salt

Can you dissolve as much solid as you want in water, or is there a limit? Will solids dissolve in liquids other than water? Will liquids dissolve in other liquids? Will gases dissolve in liquids? Does temperature have any effect on the preparation of solutions? Can you dissolve two solutes in the same solvent? Can you separate solute from solvent once a solution is made? Will stirring make a solute dissolve faster?

The following experiments will enable you to answer these questions. Be sure to label and save the solutions you make so that you can use them again.

TO STIR OR NOT TO STIR?

Place 1 teaspoon of sugar in each of two glasses that contain the same amount of water. Use a spoon to stir the water and sugar in one glass but not the other.

Does stirring make sugar dissolve faster? Will stirring make salt dissolve faster?

SUGAR IN WATER

Use a measuring cup to add 120 ml (4 fluid oz) of cold water to a clean drinking glass. Add a level teaspoon of sugar to the water. (You can use a card or ruler to sweep off crystals above the edge of the spoon.) Stir the water until all the sugar dissolves. How many teaspoons of sugar can you dissolve in the water? Can you taste the sugar in the water?

When no more solid can be dissolved in the solvent, we say the solution is *saturated*.

A prediction: See if you can predict how many teaspoons of sugar you will need to make a saturated solution using 240 ml (8 fluid oz) of water. Were you right?

A HOT SOLUTION

Repeat the experiment, but this time use 120 ml (4 fluid oz) of *hot* water. How much sugar does it take to make a saturated solution when you use hot water? Does the temperature of the water change the amount of sugar that can be dissolved in 120 ml (4 fluid oz) of water?

Pour the clear, hot solution into another glass to separate it from any dissolved sugar at the bottom of the first glass. Look at the clear, hot solution every few minutes as it cools. What happens? Taste the solid that collects at the bottom of the glass. What is it? Why do you think it comes out of solution?

SALT SOLUTIONS

How much salt (sodium chloride) will dissolve in 120 ml (4 fluid oz) of cold water? (Use kosher salt if possible. Most other table salts contain additives that may make the solution cloudy.) Can you taste the salt in the water?

Try to predict how much salt will dissolve in 240 ml (8 fluid oz) of cold water. Were you right?

Do you think more salt will dissolve in 240 ml (8 fluid oz) of hot water? Try it. Are you surprised by what you find?

2.2 What Is the Effect of

Materials:
- graduated cylinder or metric measuring cup
- hot water
- glass or beaker
- large pan
- spoon or other stirring instrument
- kosher salt
- Epsom salts
- sugar

To find out whether temperature affects solubility, you can measure the solubility of salt, Epsom salts, and sugar in hot water.

Add 50 ml of hot tap water to a glass or beaker. Place the vessel in a large pan of hot water so that the temperature of the solvent will not change as you add solute and stir the solution. What is the solubility of salt in hot water? (Express solubility in grams of solute per 100 grams of solvent.) What is the solubility of Epsom salts in hot water? Of sugar in hot water? Does temperature affect solubility? For which of the solutes you tested was solubility affected most by temperature?

Temperature on Solubility?

Science Fair Project Ideas

- Design an experiment to find the temperature at which water and saturated solutions of salt and Epsom salts freeze. How do the freezing temperatures of these liquids compare?
- Do you think a bouillon cube will dissolve faster in hot water or cold water? Design and carry out an experiment to find out.
- It is possible to determine the solubility of various salts at different temperatures, but it is not easy to do without a laboratory where temperatures can be controlled. Figure 9 (on the next page) is a graph showing the solubility of several salts at different temperatures. Use the graph to compare the solubilities of sodium chloride and potassium nitrate at different temperatures. What do you notice about their comparative solubilities?
- Which salt in Figure 9 is least soluble at room temperature (around 20°C)? Which salt shows the greatest increase in solubility with temperature? For which salt does solubility decrease as the temperature rises?

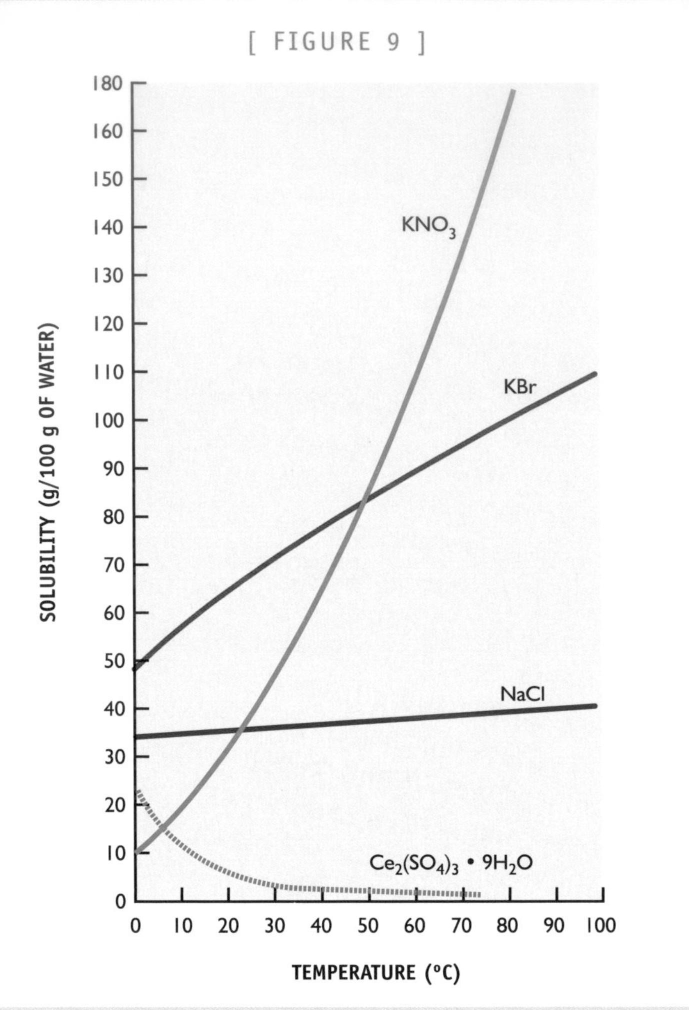

This graphs shows the solubility of four different salts at various temperatures.

KNO_3 = potassium nitrate

NaCl = sodium chloride

KBr = potassium bromide

$Ce_2(SO_4)_3 \cdot 9H_2O$ = cerium sulfate hydrate

2.3 Liquids in Liquids

Materials:

- water
- small glass or beaker
- rubbing alcohol
- spoon or other stirring device
- cooking oil
- stopwatch or clock or watch with a second hand
- liquid detergent
- eyedropper
- vial or test tube
- molasses
- small, tall jar

Pour some water into a small glass or beaker. Add about the same amount of rubbing alcohol and stir. Do alcohol and water mix to form a single phase? That is, does the mixture appear to be the same throughout?

Repeat the experiment with water and cooking oil. Do cooking oil and water mix to form a single phase?

Liquids that dissolve in one another are said to be *miscible*. Liquids that do not dissolve in one another are said to be *immiscible*. Which of the liquids you just mixed are miscible? Which are immiscible?

Half fill a glass, beaker, or test tube with tap water. Add a few drops of cooking oil to the water. How can you tell that cooking oil is less dense than water? Stir or shake the mixture and measure the time it takes for the two liquids to separate into two distinct phases.

Next, add a few drops of liquid detergent to the mixture and stir or shake. Again, measure the time it takes for the two liquids to separate into distinct phases. How does the detergent affect the rate at which the oil separates from the water? Why are detergents used to wash clothes?

Pour some rubbing alcohol into a glass or beaker. Add a few milliliters of cooking oil. Which liquid is more dense? How can you tell?

Using an eyedropper, try to make three distinct liquid layers of alcohol, cooking oil, and water in a vial or test tube. Does it matter in what order you add the liquids to the container? Which liquid forms the bottom layer? Which liquid is on top? How do the densities of water, cooking oil, and alcohol compare? How can you determine the actual density of these liquids?

In a small, tall jar, make three liquid layers, one atop the other, using water, cooking oil, and molasses. Which is the densest of these three liquids? Which is the least dense? Do you think any of the layers will eventually merge? Leave the jar for a few days. Was your prediction correct?

2.4 Exploring Emulsions

Materials:
- small jar with a screw-on lid
- vinegar
- cooking oil
- egg
- table knife
- bowl

Find a small jar with a screw-on lid that is taller than it is wide. Add vinegar to the jar until it is about 1/8 full. Then add about twice as much cooking oil. Do vinegar and cooking oil appear to be miscible?

Put the lid on the jar and shake it so as to break up the liquids and mix them together. Notice how tiny droplets of cooking oil spread throughout the liquid. Such a mixture is called an *emulsion*. Oil spills in the ocean are difficult to clean up because the wind and waves mix oil and seawater, forming an emulsion.

Let the emulsion sit for a few minutes. What happens to the two liquids over time? Why is this mixture called a temporary emulsion?

Next, separate the yolk of an egg from the white. Crack the egg at its center with a table knife. Hold the egg upright over a cereal bowl and remove the upper half of the shell. Some egg white will fall into the bowl when you remove the upper half of the shell. Then carefully pour the yolk, trying not to break it, from one half of the shell to the other several times over the bowl. As you do so, more egg white will fall into the bowl. When most of the white has been removed, pour the yolk into the mixture of oil and vinegar, put the lid on the jar, and shake it again. Let this mixture sit for a few minutes. Is this a more permanent emulsion? Why do you think the egg yolk is called an emulsifying agent? Test other foods in your refrigerator to find an even more permanent emulsion. **Always wash your hands with soap and warm water after handling raw eggs.**

2.5 Viscosity (Thickness) of

Materials:

- styrofoam cups
- small nail
- a partner
- stopwatch or clock or watch with a second hand
- sink
- pen or pencil
- notebook
- cooking oil
- rubbing alcohol
- syrup
- molasses
- soapy water

The molecules of a liquid, which are free to move about one another, interfere with one another's motion. These forces are called *viscous forces. Viscosity*, the property of being viscous, is often referred to as thickness. It is a characteristic property of liquids and can be measured in various ways. One way is to measure the time needed for different liquids to pass through a narrow opening. Liquids that are viscous take longer to pass through an opening than liquids that are less viscous. Can you explain why?

To compare the viscosities of different liquids, you can measure the time it takes the liquids to empty from a container. A Styrofoam cup makes a convenient container because you can easily make a hole in the bottom of the cup with a small nail. Place the nail inside the cup and gently push it through the center of the cup's bottom to the outside.

Hold your finger over the hole while you fill the cup to a readily identifiable level with tap water at room temperature. Have a partner with a stopwatch or a watch with a second hand say "Go!" Remove your finger when you hear "Go!" Let the water empty into a sink. At the moment the water stops flowing from the cup, say "Stop!" Your partner should then note and record the time that has elapsed since he or she started timing.

Repeat the experiment several times to be sure your results are reasonably consistent. Then calculate and record the average time for water to empty from the cup.

Repeat the experiment using cooking oil at room temperature. In this case, you will want to let the oil empty into another clean cup so that the oil can be reused. Is cooking oil more or less viscous than water?

Repeat the experiment using rubbing alcohol, syrup, molasses, and soapy water. (These liquids, too, should be captured in a clean cup so that they can be reused.)

After you have completed taking all your data, examine your results. List the liquids you have tested in order of increasing viscosity.

Science Fair Project Ideas

- Design and carry out an experiment to find out whether temperature affects viscosity.
- Design and carry out an experiment to find out whether viscosity and density are related.

2.6 Is It Solid or Liquid?

Materials:
- graduated cylinder or measuring cup
- cornstarch
- water
- disposable container
- small nail
- sheet of cardboard about 30 cm (12 in) on a side
- cover for container
- food coloring

Not all substances are easily defined as liquid or solid. To make such a substance, put 120 ml (4 oz) of cornstarch and 60 ml (2 oz) of water in a disposable pan. Use your hands to mix the water and cornstarch. You might add a few drops of food coloring to make the mass more appealing to look at.

Hold some of this strange stuff in your hand. Notice how it slips through your fingers. What happens when you try to pull it apart? When you tear it?

Use a small nail to make a hole in a sheet of cardboard. Put the strange stuff on the cardboard. Does it leak through the hole?

Play with this strange material. Test it in various ways. Does it behave like a liquid, a solid, or both?

If you want to save this substance and show it to others, store it in a covered container. If it dries, just add a little water.

The Properties of Water

WATER CAN BE FOUND AS A SOLID (ICE), A LIQUID (WATER), OR A GAS (WATER VAPOR). It has very interesting properties because of its structure. In Chapter 2, you learned that water can dissolve many substances. In fact, it is sometimes called the universal solvent. In this chapter, we will conduct experiments about surface tension, cohesion, adhesion, and capillarity.

SURFACE TENSION

Why do falling leaves float on water rather than sink below the surface? Why do they sink once they are submerged? Why do drops of water sit separately in a rounded shape on a sheet of waxed paper rather than collapsing into a film of water on the paper? Why does rain fall in separate rounded drops? Why do soap bubbles close up as they are blown free of a bubble blowing wand? *Surface tension*, a property of all liquids, is responsible for these familiar behaviors. Surface tension causes a liquid to act as if it has a thin, slightly elastic film on its surface. All bodies of water—oceans, lakes, filled bathtubs, cups of water—behave as if this thin film were covering them.

Besides explaining certain effects that we see around us, surface tension also provides useful information during certain scientific investigations. Changes in surface tension, for example, indicate the effectiveness of detergents, the nature of foaming, the presence of other chemicals, and the progress of chemical reactions.

What causes surface tension, how can it be observed, and how is it involved in other properties of water?

3.1 Can a Needle Float?

Materials:
- large bowl, fish tank, or other container filled with water
- small needle
- fork
- thread
- large straight needle (such as a darning or embroidery needle)

Would you believe that you can get a small needle to float on the surface of water even though it is made of steel? Fill a bowl or fish tank with water. (Do not use a fish tank that contains fish or has an aerator running because a calm water surface is needed.)

Try to float a small needle on top of the water. It helps if you place the needle across the tines of a fork and use the fork to gently lower the needle to the water. Observe the surface of the water touching the needle. What is different about it? How can you cause the floating needle to sink? What holds the needle up?

Thread the same needle and lower it to the water with its point down. Can you get the needle to float on its point?

Obtain a large needle, such as a darning or embroidery needle. Can you get it to float? Why is there a difference between what happens with the small and the large needles?

It is the "skin" on the surface of the water due to surface tension that holds up the small needle. The weight of the needle stretches the elastic skin. You can see the surface curving downward around the needle. Although the surface tension of water is large compared to that of most other liquids, it is still only barely strong enough to hold up the small needle. As with any elastic, the surface can be stretched only so far before it breaks. A small disturbance such as a ripple in the water is often enough to sink the needle.

When lowered point-down into the water, the needle sinks. Since it has the same weight as before, why does it sink? The answer has to do with the pressure that the needle exerts on the water. Consider that the downward pressure exerted by an object depends on two things: how heavy the object is (how much downward force it exerts) and how big the area is on which its weight rests. If the area remains the same, then the heavier the object, the greater the pressure it exerts. On the other hand, if the force is kept the same, the smaller the area upon which it acts, the greater the pressure. If the same force is spread over a much larger area, then the pressure becomes much smaller.

In the case of the needle, the area of its point is much smaller than the area of its side. For the same downward force due to the weight of the needle, the pressure will be greater on the smaller area. The area of the side of the needle is much bigger, so the needle exerts much less downward pressure on any given area when it is on its side. That is why the needle can float on its side but crashes through the surface when on its point.

Why does a larger needle sink? A large needle does not have much more surface than a smaller one. However, it can weigh much more in comparison. The greater weight over an only slightly larger area results in greater pressure, and the needle sinks.

A sharp knife easily cuts cheese or bread because the downward force acts on a very thin edge. If the edge is dull, it has a larger area, so more pressure is needed to get the knife to cut.

Liquids are made up of exceedingly tiny particles called molecules that tend to attract each other. The attraction of the identical molecules to each other in a liquid is called *cohesion*. Below the surface of a liquid, the cohesive attractions come from all around a molecule. The attractions are balanced so that a molecule isn't pulled in any one direction (see Figure 10a). However, up at the surface, things are different. The surface molecules are attracted by neighboring molecules on the sides and below, but there are no liquid molecules above to exert

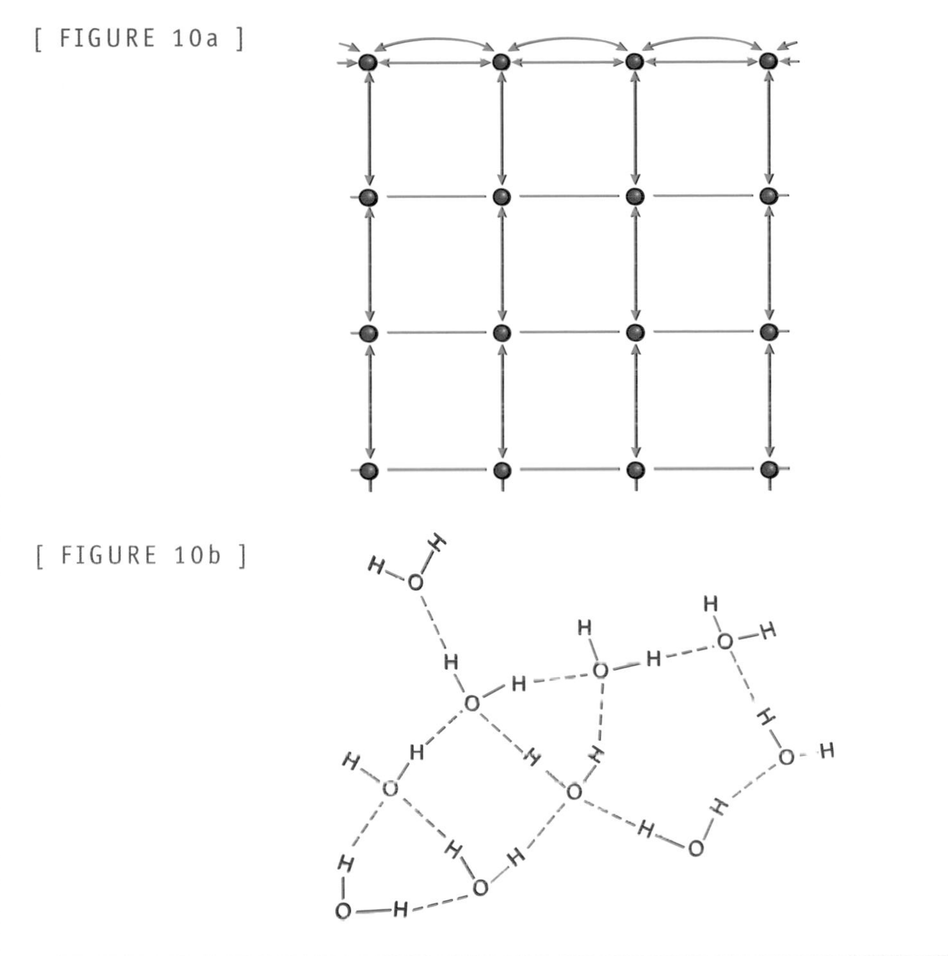

Attractions between molecules of a liquid lead to surface tension. a) In a liquid, the molecules are equally attracted to the other molecules around them except at the surface. At the surface, the attractions between molecules become stronger because there are no liquid molecules above to balance the forces. This causes surface tension. The attractive networks formed by the liquid molecules may take a variety of shapes. b) The high surface tension of water is due to its composition. The diagram shows how hydrogen atoms in each molecule are bonded strongly to their own oxygen atom (—) but are also attracted to oxygen atoms in nearby water molecules (– – – –).

a balancing attraction. It is this imbalance of forces that creates surface tension. The uneven attractions pull the surface molecules inward and toward each other to form a network of molecules at the surface that acts as a film.

Water has an unusually high surface tension, which is due to its molecular composition. Each molecule of water has one oxygen atom linked to two hydrogen atoms. The two hydrogen atoms are attracted not only to their own oxygen atom but also to nearby oxygen atoms (see Figure 10b). As a result, all the molecules of water tend to be attracted to each other more strongly than is usual for other liquids.

Surface tension is what makes it possible for insects called water striders (or pond skaters) to run across the surface of a pond. These insects have six flattened feet that help to spread out their weight. The surface is a death trap for insects that fall into the water near water striders. Trapped beneath the surface skin, the insects cannot get out. When they struggle, they agitate the water. This alerts the water striders to catch and devour them. You can see this for yourself by sitting motionless for a few minutes at the side of a shallow pond on a warm day. Use a stick to create tiny vibrations (or capture a housefly and throw it in) to attract a water strider's attention.

Science Fair Project Ideas

- Can you make a raft of needles or paper clips floating side by side? What precautions need to be taken? What happens when one paper clip touches another one or touches the wall of the container? How big can you make the raft? Can the entire surface of water in a small container be covered by paper clips butted together? What limits its size? What causes a raft to sink? Explain each of these effects in terms of surface tension.
- Try to float each of the following on water: a small straight pin, a straight pin with a large head, a large straight pin, small and large safety pins, small and large paper clips. What other objects can you cause to float in water? Based on your observations, what characteristics make an object more likely to float? Explain in terms of surface tension.
- How does the shape of a small floating object affect the appearance of the water supporting it? Try different shapes. Draw diagrams of this.

3.2 Demonstrating Surface

Materials:

- an adult
- empty food can, open at the top
- hammer
- large nail
- fish tank or any large container
- cup of water
- scissors
- sheet of paper

Obtain an empty metal can that is open at the top. **With the supervision of an adult**, hammer in a large nail to make a hole in the side of the can about an inch above the bottom.

Make two more holes near the first in a horizontal row. The holes should be evenly spaced (see Figure 11a).

Hold the can above a fish tank or large container and fill the can with water. You will see separate streams coming out of the holes.

Combine the streams into one by directing the jets of water together with your thumb and forefinger. How can you break the combined stream into single ones again?

When you pinch the jets of water, surface tension holds the combined streams together. If you brush them apart with your hand, the individual surface tensions will take over and keep the streams separate. Similarly, wetting the hairs of an artist's paintbrush allows the bristles to be smoothed to a fine point. Flicking the point with a finger splays out the bristles.

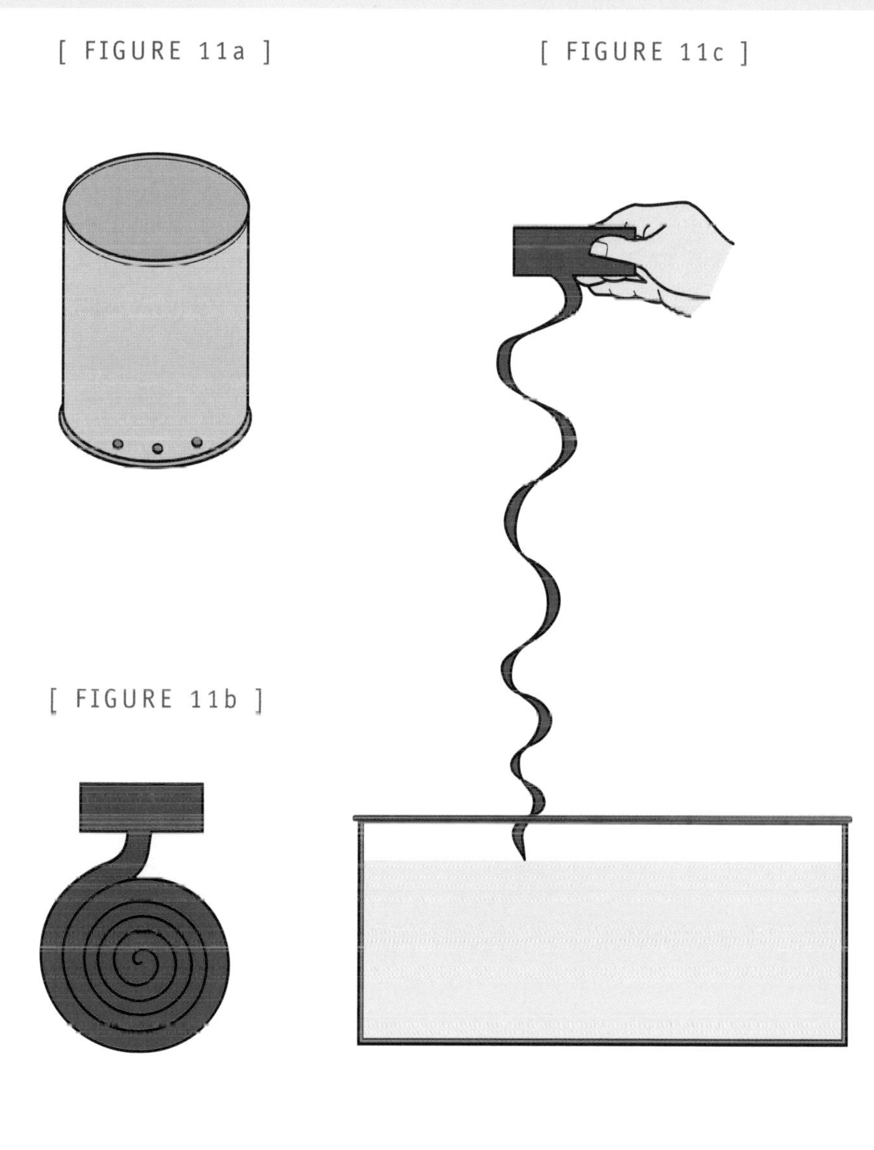

Observing surface tension. a) A can, open at top, has three evenly-spaced holes at the bottom. b) Diagram of paper spiral to be cut. c) Lower the end of the spiral to touch the surface of the water.

Try the following for another demonstration of surface tension: Cut a paper spiral with a little handle on it, as shown in Figure 11b. The handle can be about 2 inches wide and the spiral may have as many turns in it as you can make conveniently.

Hold the paper by the handle and make the other end touch the water surface. See Figure 11c. Then, pull the spiral upward.

You will find that you have to jerk the paper upward to get it free of the water. The spiral acts like a paper spring once it touches the water, and it can only be pulled free with a bounce back up. You can feel the strength of the surface tension.

COHESION, ADHESION, AND CAPILLARY ACTION

A liquid may take a huge variety of shapes. It may, for example, spread into a sheet, move in waves, swirl, flow smoothly, toss with turbulence, or scatter in drops. *Cohesion* is the property that keeps the molecules of a liquid together and, in combination with surface tension, helps to make these many shapes possible. As discussed in 3.1, cohesion is the attraction that exists between molecules in a liquid.

Adhesion is the attraction between a liquid and any solid that it touches. It is the property that causes a raindrop to stick to a windowpane and bubbles of air to adhere to the side of a bathtub. It helps liquids to stay in containers, and it is necessary for capillary action to take place. Capillary action may sound as if it is about the circulation of blood in the body and, indeed, it helps the pumping action of the heart. However, capillary action is more than that.

Capillary action moves water through narrow spaces. It moves water with dissolved nutrients through the soil so that plants can grow. It helps carry tree sap to where it is needed in a tree, even up to its very top. It is capillary action that helps a paper towel wipe up a spill and helps materials to become wet. Capillary action depends on cohesion, adhesion, and surface tension—all three of them. The experiments in the rest of this chapter will demonstrate the causes and effects of cohesion, adhesion, and capillary action.

Science Fair Project Idea

When a stream of water falls onto the center of a disk supported by a thin rod, the water spreads out from the center to fall off as a transparent sheet. It is possible to set this up so that the sheet closes back under the disk to form a bell shape. Explain this occurrence in terms of surface tension. Investigate how to change the shape of the descending sheet.

3.3 Seeing Cohesion and Adhesion

Materials:
- fish tank or any large, rectangular, transparent container filled with water
- smooth wax candle with at least 1/2-in diameter
- 2 flat glass plates (no sharp edges) or microscope slides

Cohesion and adhesion can be observed in any liquid where it contacts a solid surface.

At eye level, look at the surface of the water where it meets the corner of the fish tank. Is the water surface flat? How does it appear?

Place a wax candle halfway into the water. What does the surface of the water look like where it meets the candle?

As shown in Figure 12, the water surface curves upward where it meets the glass. Where its surface contacts the candle, the water curves downward. What is the cause of this difference?

Whether a liquid surface curves up or down on contact with a solid depends upon which is stronger, cohesion within the liquid or adhesion between the liquid and a solid. If adhesion is stronger, it pulls the liquid surface upward until the adhesion-cohesion forces are balanced. This is what happens when water meets glass. Glass is largely made up of a network of silicon and oxygen atoms. The oxygen atoms in glass attract the hydrogen atoms of the water, resulting in an adhesive force that is stronger than the cohesive force of water.

The adhesive force between water and wax, however, is not as strong as the cohesive forces within water. As a result, the water pulls away

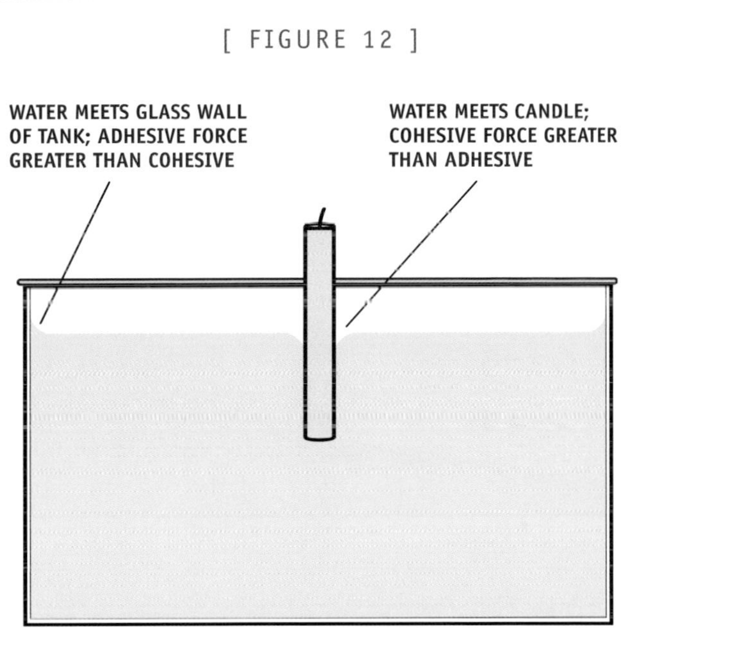

Cohesive force versus adhesive force. Where the water meets the glass wall of tank, the adhesive force is greater than the cohesive force. Where the water meets the candle, the cohesive force is greater than the adhesive force.

from the wax. It curves downward where they meet. A wax candle is made up mostly of carbon atoms strongly linked to hydrogen atoms or other carbon atoms. The wax has little, if any, attraction to water.

Wet two clean flat glass plates or microscope slides. Place one directly on the other. Now try to pull them apart. How can you separate the pieces of glass?

When you try to pull the glass plates apart, the adhesive forces between water and both glass surfaces resist you. You have to slide one of the plates away from the other until the surfaces in contact are small enough to allow you to pry them apart.

3.4 Can You Pour Water Down

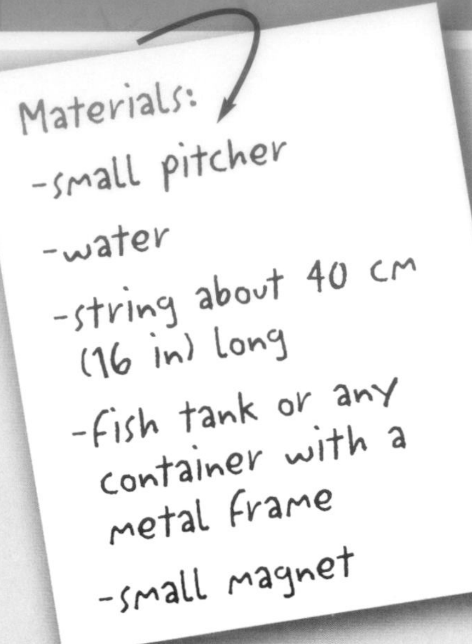

Can water be poured down a string set at a slant without spilling off?

Fill a small pitcher with water. Tie a piece of wet string about 40 cm (16 in) long to the handle. Then pass the string over the top of the pitcher and across the middle of its lip.

Set the pitcher down close to the fish tank. Pick up the free end of the string. Hold it against the inside of an upper metal frame of the fish tank. Attach it with a magnet. Move the pitcher up and hold it so that the string extends at a slant down to the tank without sagging (see Figure 13).

Pour the water slowly out. What happens?

Instead of dropping straight down, the stream of water flows along the string into the fish tank. Adhesive forces bind the descending water to the string. Cohesive forces hold the water together as it moves along the string so that drops of it do not fall away. How can you break the stream of water loose from the string?

[FIGURE 13]

Pouring water down a string

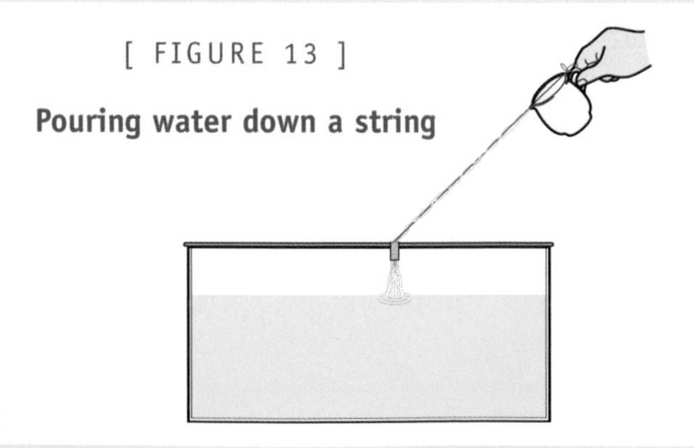

Science Fair Project Ideas

- Fish tanks often have particles of floating dirt that contaminate the water and need to be removed. A stick can be used to touch the particle and remove it from the water. Investigate what a dipstick is, what it is made of, and what shape is best for it. Explain how it works.
- Based on the curve at the solid-water interface, visually compare solids to find out how strong the adhesive force is. Try materials such as glass, steel, porcelain (as in a mug), polystyrene, Teflon, paraffin, Plexiglas, and others. List the materials in approximate order of their adhesive strength at the water-solid interface.
- The angle that a liquid forms at the interface with its container is called the contact angle. You can roughly measure the contact angle by using a protractor; a magnifying glass helps. What is the size of the contact angle for the water-glass interface? Compare the adhesive strength exerted on water by other solids besides glass by measuring the contact angles. List them in order of their adhesive strength for water. Consider researching the composition of the other solids to explain the differences.
- Compare the adhesive force at the glass-liquid interface for different liquids such as water, alcohol, glycerol, and cooking oil based on the contact angle. List them in order of the adhesive force. Does the contact angle give you information about their cohesive forces?
- Does the adhesive force at the glass-water interface change with temperature? Design an experiment to investigate.

3.5 Can You Make Water Flow

Materials:

- any large container, filled with water
- bucket or large jar
- transparent plastic flexible tubing at least 60 cm (2 ft) long
- optional: giant dropper (baster)
- optional: clamp

Use a large container or a fish tank without fish in it for this experiment.

Place a large jar or bucket next to and below the water-filled container. Obtain a piece of flexible tubing at least 60 cm (2 ft) long. Fill it completely with water. The tubing should have no air bubbles in it.

There are several ways to completely fill the tubing. Here are two of them.

1. The easiest way is to use a clean giant dropper. It is sold as a baster in the kitchen section of grocery, hardware, or discount stores. Place one end of the tubing into the water-filled container with the other end hanging out. Squeeze the bulb of the dropper to empty it of air and place the tip into the water in the tank. Release the bulb so that the dropper fills with water. Push the tip of the dropper into the end of the tubing that is outside the tank. Squeeze the bulb to fill the tube completely with water and let it drive out all the air. Pinch the tubing to close it tightly below the dropper or close it with a clamp. Disconnect the dropper from the tubing. There should be no air bubbles in the tubing.
2. Attach one end of the tubing to a faucet and place the other end at the bottom of the partly-filled container. Run a stream of water into the tubing until no more air comes out. Pinch tightly or clamp the faucet end of the tubing. Leave the other end under water in the container. Disconnect the tubing from the faucet.

At this point, one end of the tubing is open at the bottom of the tank and the other is outside the tank and clamped closed. Pull the closed end so that the tubing extends over the top of the tank and down into the jar below. Open the end in the jar.

Water will flow from the tank up the tube and down the other side. If it doesn't, you probably have an air bubble in the tubing. Refill it and repeat the process. Once the water is flowing, you have made a siphon (see Figure 14). Why does a siphon work?

The explanation involves a combination of causes. Although it is often believed that the water is pushed over the top by air pressure, this is disproved by the simple fact that a siphon works in a vacuum. A siphon works after you have provided the initial energy needed to get the water up the tubing and over the top of the tank. The weight of water in the tubing going into the jar is greater than that of the water in the shorter part of the tubing that goes to the tank. It is this imbalance of weight that powers the continuing flow of the siphon. Cohesive forces keep the water from breaking apart as it flows over the arch. Adhesive forces help by pulling the water to the sides. The siphon will work as long as the water level in the catch bucket is below the water level in the tank. Once the catch bucket is nearly full, lift it up until the siphon stops to prevent a mess.

[FIGURE 14]

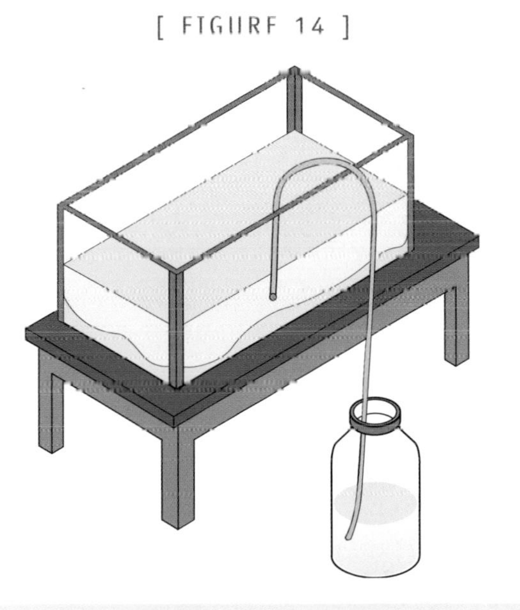

An operating siphon

3.6 Experimenting With a

Materials:

- fish tank without fish in it or other large container, filled with water
- bucket or large jar
- transparent plastic flexible tubing about 150 cm (5 ft) long
- optional: giant dropper (baster)

Completely fill with water a length of tubing about 150 cm (5 ft) long, as described in Experiment 3.5, and start a siphon operating from a filled fish tank into a bucket or jar.

Lift up the bucket or jar into which the siphon is emptying until it is above the water level in the fish tank. Be sure that the ends of the tubing remain underwater throughout. What do you observe? After a short time, lower the jar until it is below the fish tank. Which way does the water move now? Try siphoning back and forth.

Raise the jar until the water level in the jar is slightly above the water level in the fish tank. How long does the siphon continue to operate?

Raise the jar again until it is completely above the fish tank. How long does the siphon continue to operate? When it stops, what do you observe has happened to the column of water on each side of the siphon?

Restart your siphon. Does the siphon work if the tubing droops below the catch bucket before entering it? Does the siphon work if the tubing has some loops in it above the tank? Can you make the siphon work with the 150-cm length of tubing looped as high up as possible?

What happens to the siphon if the end in the fish tank flips above the water?

When the jar is momentarily lifted above the fish tank, the siphon reverses direction, going from the jar to the fish tank. When the jar is placed below the fish tank, the siphon again reverses direction, this time withdrawing water from the fish tank. Then, when the water level in the jar is set higher than that in the fish tank, the siphon continues until both water levels are equal. At that point it stops, but it can be restarted if the jar is raised or lowered.

When the jar is raised above the fish tank and allowed to continue operating, its action continues until the jar is empty. At that point the water column breaks, and the siphon stops.

An operating siphon continues to work no matter how many loops are made in the tubing. The siphon works with a higher arch, too. If the end of the tubing in the fish tank flips out of the water, the column of water is broken, and the siphon stops operating.

If you were to allow the siphon to continue operating, it would empty the fish tank. This is probably the safest way to empty a fish tank. Of course, you would need to empty it into a larger container than the jar.

Science Fair Project Ideas

In all experiments that require working from a window, roof, ladder, or stairwell, be sure to have adult supervision.

- Construct a siphon that runs from the fish tank to the ceiling and back again. Does it continue to operate? Run a siphon hose around the room before feeding it into the receiving container. Does it still continue to operate? Why?
- Does the speed of flow of a siphon depend upon the diameter of the tubing? Make a hypothesis and conduct experiments to test it.
- Design experiments to determine whether the speed of flow of a siphon depends upon the maximum height above the water surface in the tank that the siphon tubing reaches.
- Make a hypothesis and design experiments to find whether differences in height between the water levels in the upper and receiving containers in a siphon affect the speed of flow. Graph the rate of flow versus the difference in height and interpret the results.
- Design an experiment to check whether any outside air pressure is needed to operate a siphon. To explain the results, it may be helpful to look in physics books and physics magazines for information on the topic.
- A modern toilet uses a siphon mechanism. Make a diagram showing how it works. What determines the height of the siphon? Suggest modifications and the possible consequences.

3.7 Capillary Action

Materials:
- fish tank or any large, rectangular, transparent glass container filled with water
- 2 glass tubes, one with an opening about 0.6 cm (0.25 in) wide and one with a wider opening

Vertically lower a glass tube with a 0.6-cm (0.25-in) opening until it is partway into the water in a fish tank. Look at the water surface inside the tube. Is it flat? How does its level compare with that of the water outside the tube?

Repeat the observation but use glass tubing with a wider opening. Compare the results.

When glass tubing is lowered into water, the water rises until it is higher inside the tube than outside the tube. Not only is the column of water higher, but the water is even higher at the edges all around. The increase in height is not as great when the tube is wider. The term used to describe this occurrence is *capillary action*.

Capillary action is not a simple phenomenon. Essentially, it is due to a combination of adhesion, surface tension, and cohesion. In a glass tube, adhesive forces act from all sides on the narrow column of water. The adhesive forces pull the water upward along the glass. Cohesion pulls the molecules of water together so that the water rises as a column without a break. Surface tension keeps the surface from breaking. Gravity pulls the water downward. The water rises until the upward adhesive pull is balanced by the downward force of gravity on the water: the water's weight.

The narrower the glass tube, the higher the water goes (see Figure 15). This is because the adhesive force in a narrow tube increases at a faster rate than the weight of the water does. Can you think of any ways that you depend upon capillary action? Do you think plants use capillary action to move water up their stems?

[FIGURE 15]

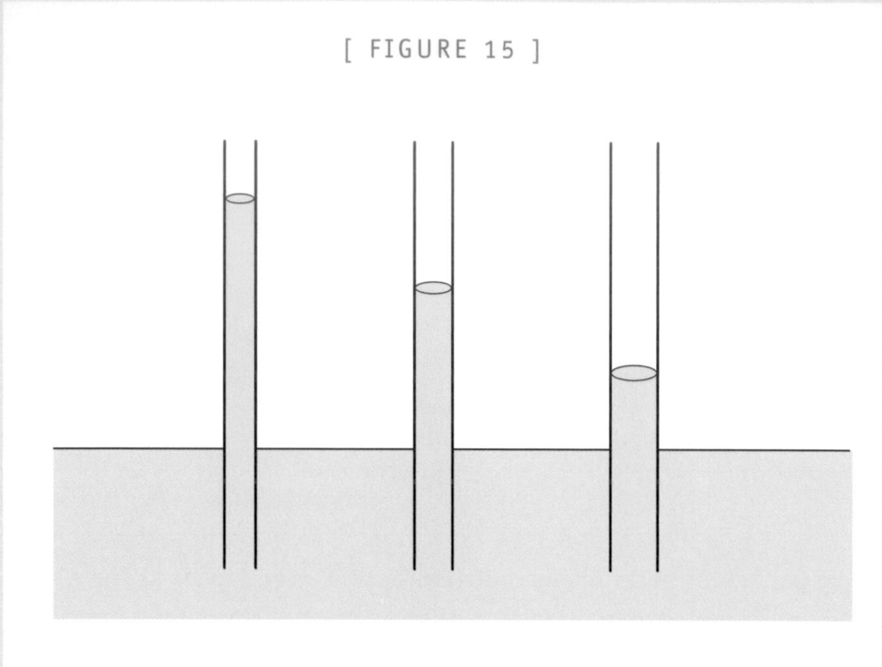

Capillary action in narrow tubes of different diameters

The Properties of Gases

YOU PROBABLY ALREADY KNEW SOMETHING ABOUT LIQUIDS AND SOLIDS even before you did the experiments in the previous chapters. This is because you see and touch liquids and solids every day. You may know less about gases because you cannot see them. Air is made up of gases. Even though we can't see, smell, or taste air, we can feel it. When the wind blows, you feel something moving over your skin. When you ride your bike or run, you feel something pushing against the skin on your face. Sometimes you can hear air as it rushes from a pump or hose. You can also hear the wind howl.

We think of gases as light substances and solids as heavy. However, a roomful of air might weigh 40 kilograms or more. A solid coin, such as a nickel, weighs only 5 grams. If we weigh *equal* volumes of a solid and a gas, their differences are more apparent. A cubic centimeter of nickels weighs 8.9 grams. The same volume of air weighs only 0.0012 grams.

In Chapter 1, you measured the volumes and masses of solids and liquids. You also found a way to measure the volume of a gas that does not dissolve in water. Measuring the mass of a gas is more complicated because, as you will see, its mass is affected by the air in which it is weighed. Because gases are hard to see, we will begin by collecting evidence that gases exist.

4.1 What Is in an "Empty" Jar?

Materials:
- basin or sink
- widemouthed jar
- water
- small cork or piece of Styrofoam

Fill a basin or sink with water. Take an "empty" jar or bottle, turn it upside down, and push its open mouth down into the water, as shown in Figure 16a. Slowly push the jar deeper into the water. Does water move into the jar as you push it into the water? Does the water level outside the jar stay even with the water level inside the jar? What evidence do you have that there is something inside the jar?

Keeping the mouth of the jar underwater, slowly turn the jar on its side (see Figure 16b). Watch the mouth of the bottle closely. As water enters the jar, do you see anything coming out of the jar? Do you have evidence that a gas (perhaps air) was in the jar?

Put a small cork or a small piece of Styrofoam on the surface of a water-filled basin or sink. Turn an "empty" widemouthed jar upside down and lower it over the cork. Then push the jar down into the water. Do the cork and the water on which it is floating remain level with the water outside the jar? What evidence do you have that something really is inside the "empty" jar?

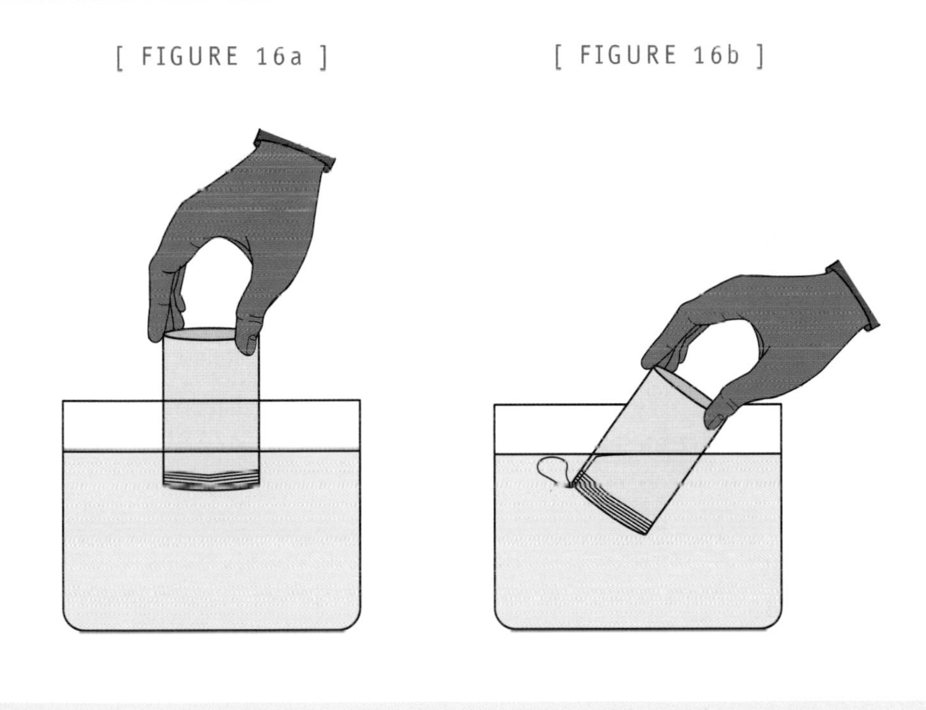

16a) Push the mouth of an "empty" jar down into a container of water. Is anything in the jar? b) Keeping the mouth of the jar underwater, slowly turn the jar on its side. What do you see coming out of the jar?

4.2 Air Pushing Water Out of

Materials:
- small plastic bag
- basin or sink
- water
- 2 widemouthed jars or bottles
- a partner

Hold open the mouth of a small plastic bag and drag it a short distance across a room. Twist shut the open end of the bag and hold it closed. Use your other hand to gently squeeze the part of the bag that has been sealed off. How do you know you have captured something in the bag? Perhaps that something is air.

Have a partner hold the sealed bag while you fill a basin or sink with water. Put a widemouthed jar or bottle under the water. Turn the jar so that it fills with water. Have your partner hold the water-filled jar upside down with its mouth underwater as shown in Figure 17. Hold the closed plastic bag so that its mouth is under the mouth of the jar. Untwist the bag and gently squeeze the gas in the bag. What comes out of the bag? What happens to the water inside the jar?

Find a second widemouthed jar similar to the one you just used. Place one jar in the basin or sink and fill it with water. Turn and hold it so that it is upside down and remains full with its mouth underwater (see Figure 18a). Turn the second empty jar upside down. Push its open mouth down into the water. As you found before, air in the jar prevents water from entering. Now carefully tip the second jar so that air coming out of its mouth can enter the water-filled jar above it (see Figure 18b). Notice how the air from the second jar displaces the water in the first one you are holding upside down.

EVIDENCE OF GASES

From the experiments you have done, you have good evidence that air exists. You have seen that there is something in a jar that appears to be empty. You know something is there, because when you push its open

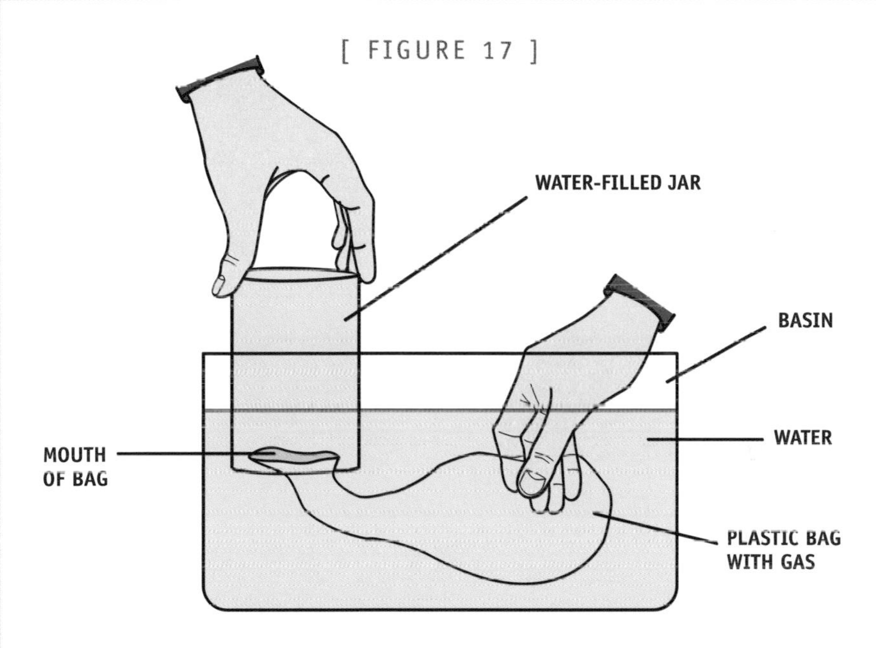

A gas from a plastic bag displaces water in a jar.

mouth down into water, water does not enter the jar. Air fills the space in the jar, and water cannot get in.

If you pull an open plastic bag through the space around you, you can close off the bag and feel that there is something in the bag. The gas in the bag resists being squeezed; it takes up space inside the bag. If you open the bag, you can squeeze the gas into a water-filled jar. The gas will displace (push out) the water from the jar.

Chemists weigh air by using a pump to remove air from a strong glass jar. This creates a vacuum inside the jar. A valve is used to close off the jar so that no air can enter. The truly empty jar is weighed, and the weight is recorded. The valve is then opened so that air can enter the jar. When the jar is reweighed, it is found to weigh more. If the jar has a volume of 1.0 l, its weight will increase by about 1.2 g.

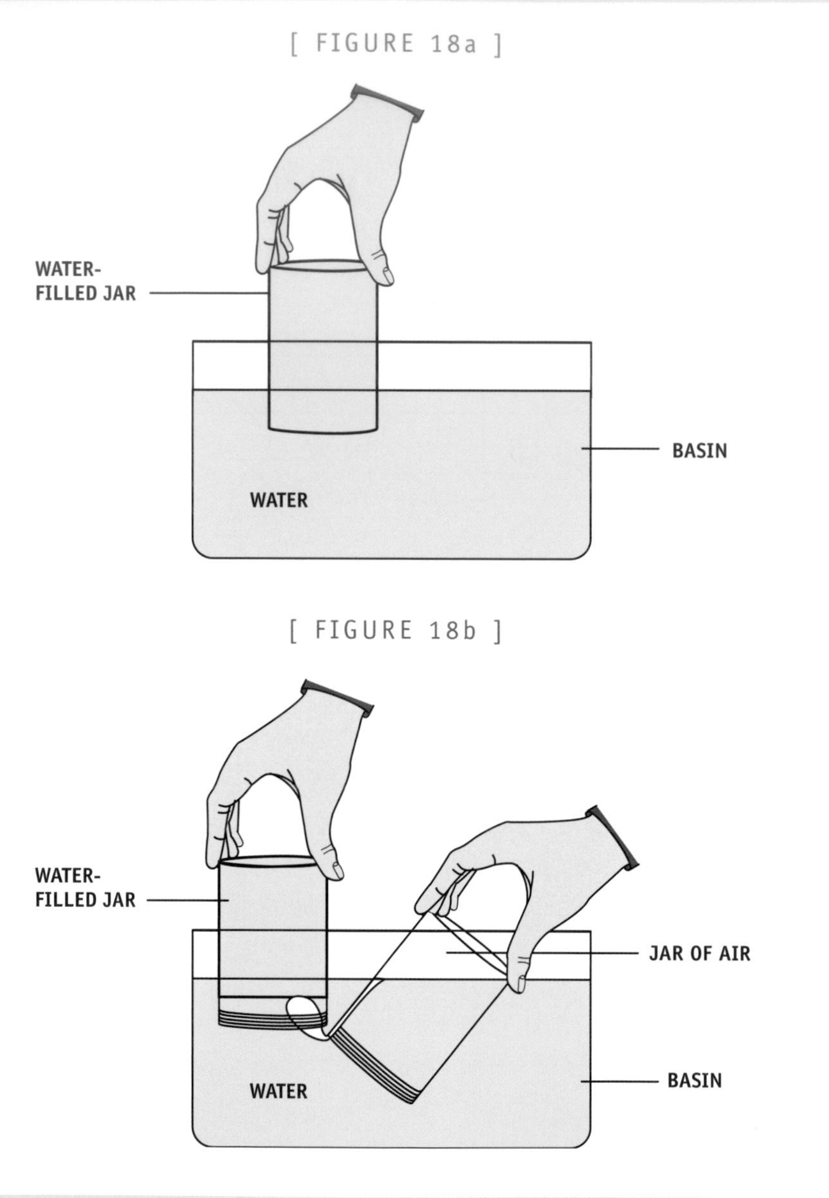

18a) A water-filled jar is shown with its mouth underwater. b) Air from one jar displaces water in another.

The weight of 1.0 l of air will be affected by its pressure and temperature. A liter of warm air weighs less than a liter of cold air. Air weighed on a mountaintop, where the pressure is less, will not weigh as much as air weighed at sea level.

The results of some experiments in which different gases were weighed in a room where the pressure was 1.0 atmosphere (76 cm, or 30 in of mercury, or 1.013 bar) and the temperature was 20°C (68°F) are shown in Table 1. The weights are given in grams (g). The weights of the gases were found by first weighing a 1.0-liter flask from which all the air had been removed. A gas was then allowed to enter the flask. The flask was sealed and reweighed. The weight of the gas was found by subtracting the weight of the empty flask from the weight of the gas-filled flask.

TABLE 1

Weights of 1.0 liter of several different gases

Gas	*Weight of 1.0 liter*
Air	1.20 g
Argon	1.66 g
Carbon dioxide	1.83 g
Helium	0.17 g
Hydrogen	0.08 g
Nitrogen	1.17 g
Oxygen	1.33 g
Sulfur dioxide	2.67 g

Which of the gases in Table 1 is the heaviest per liter (densest)? Which gas in the table weighs the least per liter (least dense)? Which gases are heavier (more dense) than air? Which gases are lighter (less dense) than air?

4.3 Is Carbon Dioxide Heavier

Materials:

- an adult
- laboratory balance from your school or balance built in Experiment 1.3
- antacid tablets (the kind that fizz in water)
- water
- measuring cup or medicine cup
- small, clear flask or bottle (An empty aspirin bottle that holds 250 tablets works well.)
- 3 balloons about 23 cm (9 in) or larger of different colors
- paper towels
- bicycle tire pump

Table 1 indicates that an equal volume of carbon dioxide is heavier than air. To see if that's true, you can compare the weights of equal volumes of air and carbon dioxide.

You can make some carbon dioxide by dropping antacid tablets into water. The antacid reacts with the water to form bubbles of carbon dioxide gas that you can collect.

Put about 30 ml (1 oz) of water in a small, clear flask or bottle. (A clean, empty aspirin bottle that holds 250 tablets works fine.) Break two antacid tablets in half. Drop them into the water and pull the neck of a balloon over the top of the flask. The carbon dioxide gas will blow up the balloon as the gas is produced in the flask.

Gently swirl the flask to free as many carbon dioxide bubbles as possible. When the reaction is over, **ask an adult** to remove the balloon from the flask and quickly tie a knot at the neck of the balloon. Dry the mouth of the balloon with a paper towel.

Use a bicycle tire pump to fill a second balloon of the same size but a different color with air. Inflate the balloon to the same size as the one with carbon dioxide. Again **ask an adult** to tie a knot at the neck of the balloon. Hang both balloons from opposite ends of the meterstick balance or weigh them separately on a laboratory balance. Is carbon dioxide heavier (more dense) than air?

You may have heard that the gas you exhale (breathe out) from your lungs contains carbon dioxide. Do you think lung air is as heavy (dense) as carbon dioxide? Do you think it is heavier (more dense) than air?

You can find out by blowing your lung air into a third balloon of a different color than the first two. Inflate it to the same size as the air- and carbon dioxide-filled balloons. Then tie a knot at the neck of the balloon as before. Use a paper towel to wipe off any saliva that might be in the neck of the balloon.

Compare the weights of the three balloons on your meterstick balance or on a laboratory balance. Is lung air as heavy (dense) as an equal volume of carbon dioxide? Is it heavier (more dense) than an equal volume of air?

4.4 Measuring the Mass of Air

Materials:
- balance from Experiment 1.3 or appropriate substitute
- plastic bags (1 gallon or larger) and very large plastic bags such as trash bags
- twist ties

Try to find the mass of some air by weighing it. If you are using the balance described in Experiment 1.3, follow the directions below. If you are using a different kind of balance, such as an electronic or triple-beam balance, you need to weigh a plastic bag (1 gallon or larger) and twist tie when the bag is empty and again when it is filled with air and sealed with the twist tie.

To use the balance you built in Experiment 1.3, remove the pans and use twist ties to hang two identical plastic bags (1 gallon or larger) from opposite ends of the balance. Both bags should be collapsed; that is, neither bag should hold any air. If the balance beam is not level, move the small lump of clay along the beam until it is. Now remove the bag from one end of the beam and drag it through the air to fill it with gas. Then hang the air-filled bag back on the balance. Does the air appear to have any mass?

Perhaps there was too little air to affect the balance. Try using a much larger plastic bag, such as a trash bag. Does a larger volume of air appear to have any mass?

Does air really have no mass? How can it be that the air you feel pushing against you when the wind blows, when you ride your bicycle, or when you hold your hand out a moving car window has no mass? Perhaps the answer can be found by doing a similar experiment with water.

4.5 Measuring the Mass of Water in Air and in Water

Materials:
- balance you built in Experiment 1.3 or a spring balance
- plastic sandwich bags
- water
- twist ties
- a partner, if you use the balance you built in Experiment 1.3
- pail

You know that water has mass; you may have weighed it before. But did you ever weigh water *in water*? To find the mass of water in water, you can use either the balance you built in Experiment 1.3 or a spring balance.

If you use a spring balance, partially fill a plastic sandwich bag with water. Twist the top of the bag to close off the water. Be sure there are no air bubbles trapped with the water, then seal it shut with a twist tie. Use the end of the twist tie to hang the bag of water from a spring balance, as shown in Figure 19a. What is the mass of the bag, the twist tie, and the water?

Now lower the bag of water hanging from the spring balance into a pail of water (see Figure 19b). What is the mass of the water, bag, and twist tie when weighed in water?

If you use the balance you built in Experiment 1.3, you will need a partner to help you. Obtain two identical plastic sandwich bags and twist ties. Be sure they have the same mass by hanging them from the paper clips at opposite ends of your balance. If they are not quite the same, move the lump of clay until the beam is level. Next, fill one plastic bag with water. Twist the top of the bag to close off the water. Be sure that no air bubbles are trapped inside, then seal it shut with a twist tie. Have

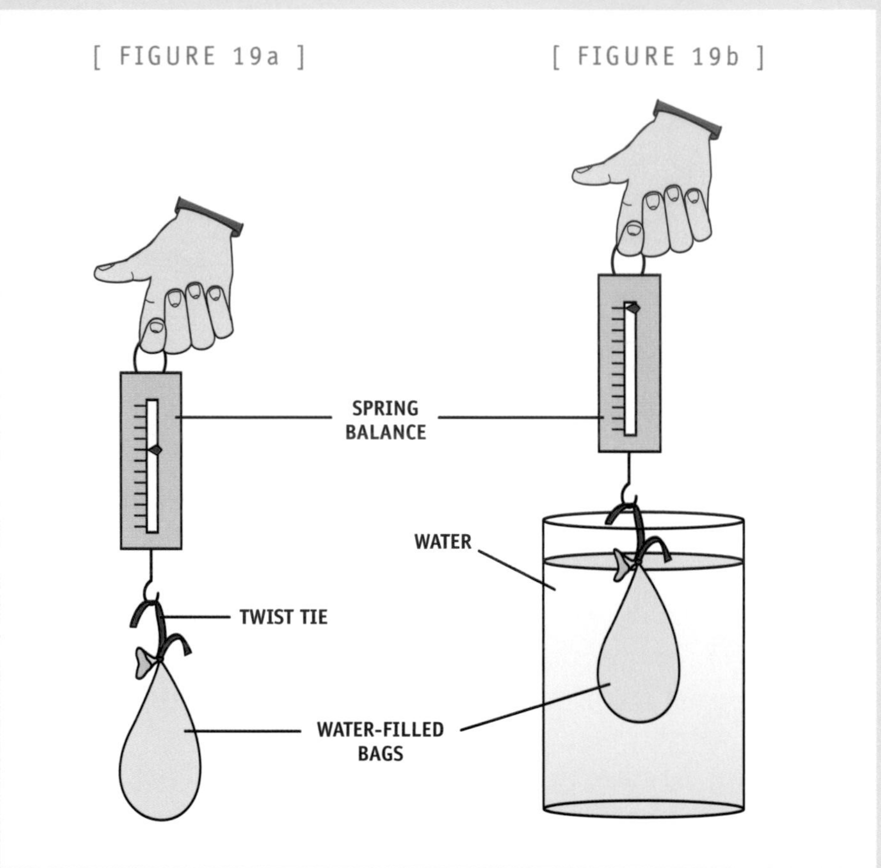

19a) A water-filled bag is weighed in air. b) The same bag is weighed while submerged in water.

your partner hold the balance beam while you hang the bag of water from one end of the balance. Have your partner continue to keep the balance beam level while you raise a pail of water under the bag of water until it is submerged, as shown in Figure 20. Then have your partner release the beam. What is the mass of water when weighed in water? How does it compare with the mass of air when weighed in air?

ARCHIMEDES AND BUOYANCY

The Greek philosopher Archimedes (287–212 B.C.) was one of the few Greek philosophers who actually did experiments. One of his experiments occurred quite unexpectedly.

Archimedes had been trying to figure out a way to measure the volume of an irregularly shaped object. The irregular shape was the king's crown. The king thought he might have been cheated. He had asked Archimedes

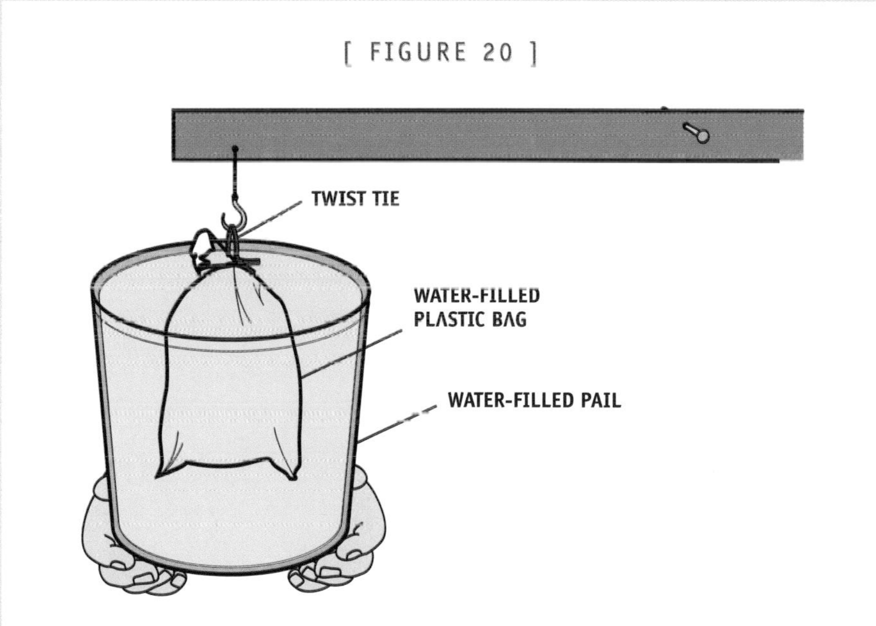

Weighing a water-filled plastic bag in water

to find out whether the crown was made of pure gold. To find the density of the crown, and thus determine if it was solid gold, Archimedes needed to know its volume.

While getting into his bath, Archimedes suddenly realized that a solid object displaces its own volume when submerged in a liquid. According to legend, he leaped from the bath and ran naked through the streets, shouting, "*Eureka! Eureka!*" In Greek, *eureka* means "I have found it!"

Archimedes' realization that the volume of a solid could be found by immersing it in a liquid led him to another discovery. His careful experiments revealed that a solid object in a liquid is buoyed up (lifted) by a force equal to the weight of the liquid it displaces. Later experiments showed that gases, too, provide buoyancy.

His discovery about buoyancy is known today as Archimedes' Principle: *A body in a fluid (liquid or gas) is buoyed up (lifted) by a force equal to the weight of the fluid it displaces.*

4.6 Measuring the Mass of Gases

Materials:

- balance you made in Experiment 1.3 or electronic or triple-beam balance that can detect hundredths of a gram
- twist ties
- 2 identical large balloons
- air pump, such as one used to pump bicycle tires or balls used in sports
- football, soccer ball, or other inflatable ball
- needle valve used to inflate balls used in sports

As you have seen, air appears to have no mass when weighed in air. And water appears to have no mass when weighed in water. Archimedes' Principle explains why air weighed in air and water weighed in water both appear to be weightless. Each is buoyed up by the weight of the fluid it displaces. Since a volume of air displaces its own volume, it is buoyed up by its own weight and so appears to be weightless. Similarly, water weighed in water displaces its own volume and so is buoyed up by its own weight.

You know that water has mass because you can weigh it in air. The buoyancy effect of the air is much less than the weight of the water. Is there any way to determine the mass of a volume of air?

One way might be to pack more air into a volume than it normally holds. That is, you could increase the air pressure inside a closed container and see if its mass increases. If your balance is quite sensitive, you might be able to detect the weight of air in a balloon. You know that the pressure of the air inside a balloon is greater than the pressure outside, because when you release the balloon, the air comes rushing out.

Use twist ties to hang two large, identical but empty balloons from opposite ends of the balance you built in Experiment 1.3. Use an air pump, such as one used to pump bicycle tires or balls used in sports, to force air into one of the balloons. (Why shouldn't you use air from your lungs for this experiment?) Tie a knot at the neck of the balloon. Hang that balloon back on the balance. Can you detect any increase in mass?

Another approach would be to place an empty balloon on the pan of an electronic or triple-beam balance that can detect hundredths of a gram. Force air into the balloon with an air pump, tie it off, and then see if the balloon's mass has increased.

With a football, soccer ball, or any inflatable ball, you can really increase the pressure significantly. You can put two or three times as much air into these volumes as would be there normally. Begin by weighing the ball when no more air will come out of it through a needle valve you stick in the ball. The air inside the ball will then be at the same pressure as the air outside. The ball is now deflated, but not compressed. You should not squeeze the remaining air out because you want the ball's volume to be constant. Remember: An object is buoyed by a force equal to the weight of the fluid (in this case air) it displaces.

Now use the needle valve and air pump to add air to the ball until it is inflated to its recommended pressure or until it feels very firm. Then weigh it again. Can you detect any change in the mass of the ball? If you can, you have succeeded in showing that air has mass.

4.7 Finding the Density of Carbon Dioxide Gas

Materials:

- antacid tablet (the kind that fizzes in water)
- balance you built in Experiment 1.3
- twist tie
- test tube
- graduated cylinder or metric measuring cup
- heavy drinking glass
- water
- pen or pencil
- notebook
- rubber tubing about 50 cm (20 in) long
- one-hole rubber stopper to fit test tube
- glass tube about 10 cm (4 in) long to fit into rubber stopper
- large bottle (500 mL–1 liter [1 pint–1 quart])
- plastic pail
- square piece of cardboard or glass to cover mouth of bottle

As you have seen, antacid tablets react with water to form carbon dioxide. If you weigh the water and antacid tablet before and after the reaction, any loss of mass should be due to the carbon dioxide gas that escapes. By collecting the carbon dioxide, you can measure its volume. Knowing the mass and volume of the gas, you can calculate its density.

To carry out this experiment, break an antacid tablet in half and place the pieces on the pan of the balance you built in Experiment 1.3. Use a twist tie to hang a test tube with about 10 ml of water in it from the paper clip to which the pan is attached (see Figure 21a). The test tube should be about 1/4 to 1/3 full. Record the combined mass of tablet and test tube.

Next, set up the apparatus shown in Figure 21b. The test tube can be supported by a heavy drinking glass. Fill the large bottle with water and fill the pail about one-third of the way with water. Cover the mouth of the bottle with a cardboard square. Hold the square against the bottle as you turn the bottle upside down and put its mouth under the water in the pail. Place the rubber tubing (about 50 cm long) inside and at the top of the large bottle of water. Drop the pieces of tablet into the water in the test tube; then immediately insert the one-hole rubber stopper into the mouth of the test tube. The glass tube and the rubber tubing now connect two containers. Carbon dioxide gas will be produced in the test tube as the tablet reacts with water. The gas will travel through the tubing to the bottle, where it will collect as it displaces water from the bottle.

Let the reaction proceed for about 10 minutes. By that time the reaction will be nearly complete.

Remove the rubber tube that extends to the top of the bottle before you remove the rubber stopper from the test tube. Otherwise, air may flow through the tubing into the bottle.

Cover the mouth of the bottle with a square piece of cardboard or glass and remove the bottle from the pail. How can you use a graduated cylinder or metric measuring cup to find the volume of gas that was

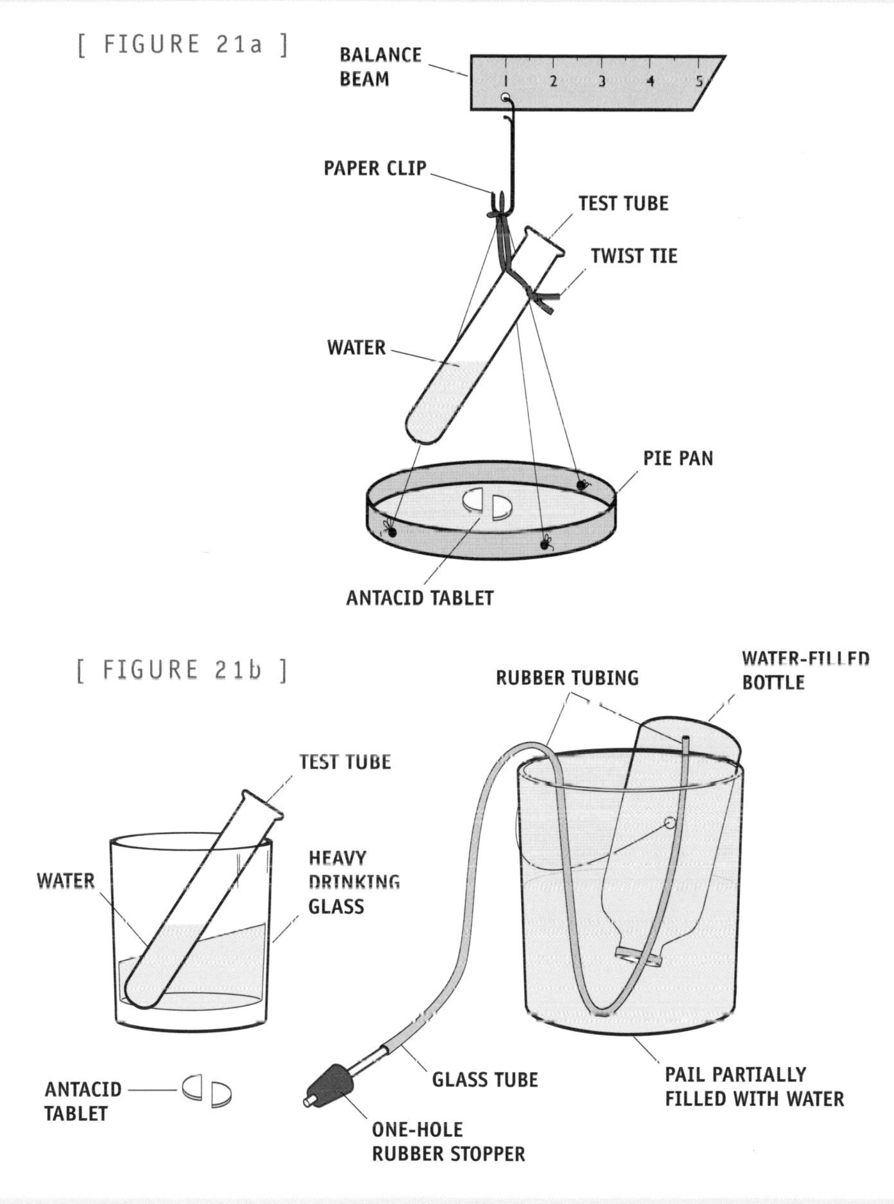

The apparatus shown here, together with a balance and graduated cylinder, will enable you to find the density of carbon dioxide.

produced? How can you find the mass of the gas? Record your data in a notebook.

Using the recorded mass and volume of the gas, determine the density of the carbon dioxide. What assumptions have you made in arriving at the density of carbon dioxide?

Science Fair Project Idea

Investigate how you might find the density of other gases using a technique similar to the one you used for carbon dioxide. After you have developed a plan, conduct your experiments **under the supervision of an adult.**

Chapter 5

Physical and Chemical Changes

JUST AS GLUES CAN FORM PHYSICAL OR CHEMICAL BONDS, other substances can go through physical or chemical changes. When carbon dioxide gas leaves a liquid, for example, physical change occurs because no new substance is formed. In a chemical change, a new substance is created.

Boiling is a type of physical change. While the form of the substance changes, no new substance is made. A physical change is also reversible. At a high enough temperature (the boiling point), liquid completely changes to a gas. At a low enough temperature (the freezing point), liquid changes to a solid. The change of a substance from solid to liquid, liquid to solid, liquid to gas, gas to liquid, and so on is known as a change of state. Boiling and freezing points can increase when pressure increases. Under normal pressure, pure water boils at 100°C (212°F) and freezes at 0°C (32°F). If the pressure is increased, such as in a pressure cooker, the boiling point increases; the water reaches temperatures higher than 100°C (212°F). Adding substances to a liquid can also change the boiling and freezing points of the liquid. In a mixture such as sugar water, for example, the freezing point is lower and the boiling point is higher than for the pure liquid.

In a boiling liquid, bubbles of gas form and escape from the liquid's surface. In a carbonated beverage, bubbles can form at room temperature. Just because there are bubbles in the beverage does not mean that the beverage is boiling. Something different causes the bubbles to form in the drink. Under pressure, water molecules surround carbon dioxide (CO_2) gas. Whenever a bottle or can of carbonated soda is opened, the volume of the dissolved CO_2 increases, and the gas makes bubbles and escapes from the liquid. When a carbonated beverage is bubbling, you know that CO_2 is leaving the liquid.

Chemical changes are different from physical changes. In a chemical change, a chemical reaction takes place and one substance is changed to another substance. A chemical change is not reversible. An example of a chemical change is the formation of rust. Rust is a combination of iron and oxygen. It forms when iron reacts with water. Rust is a different substance than any of the original substances. Acids can react with rust and other metal oxides to cause further chemical changes to occur.

5.1 Making Solids Disappear

Materials:

- an adult
- science teacher
- graduated cylinder or metric measuring cup
- room-temperature water
- glasses
- measuring teaspoon
- spoon
- sugar
- salt (kosher salt if possible)
- coffee filters
- funnel
- other solids such as baking soda, Epsom salts, flavored drink crystals, flour, and cornstarch
- other liquids such as rubbing alcohol, vinegar, and cooking oil
- dry ice (see telephone book for a source)
- heavy gloves
- flask or small bottle like the one used to produce carbon dioxide in Experiment 4.3
- balloon
- balance
- iodine crystals
- fume hood

Use a graduated cylinder or metric measuring cup to pour 100 ml of room-temperature water into each of two glasses. Add a level teaspoonful of sugar to one of the glasses of water and stir the mixture. What happens to the solid sugar?

Repeat the experiment using a level teaspoonful of kosher salt. (Kosher salt is recommended because it does not have added substances that make water cloudy.) Stir the mixture. What happens to the salt?

As discussed in Chapter 2, when solids disappear in liquids, we say that a solute (solid) has dissolved in a solvent (liquid) to form a solution. Use a spoon to remove a tiny bit of liquid from the sugar solution. Place the liquid on your tongue. Can you taste the dissolved sugar?

Repeat the experiment with the salt solution. Can you taste the dissolved salt?

Perhaps you can separate the solute from the solvent by pouring the solution through a filter. Fold a coffee filter to make a conical filter, as shown in Figure 22. (Note: If you use a #2 or #4 filter, you do not have to fold it to fit the funnel.) Place the filter in a funnel. Pour some of the sugar solution into the filter and collect the liquid that comes through in a small glass. After all the liquid has flowed through the filter, can you see any sugar on the filter paper? Can you still taste sugar in the liquid that came through the filter paper?

Do you think you can separate salt from the water in which it dissolved by pouring it through a filter? Try it! Were you right?

Add 100 ml of sugar to 100 ml of water and stir. Do you get 200 ml of solution? Can you explain the results you obtain?

Solids that dissolve are said to be soluble. Solids that do not dissolve are said to be insoluble. Sugar and salt are soluble in water. What other substances are soluble in water? You might try baking soda (sodium bicarbonate), Epsom salts (magnesium sulfate), flavored drink crystals, flour, and cornstarch. Which of these solids are soluble in water? Are any of them insoluble?

[FIGURE 22]

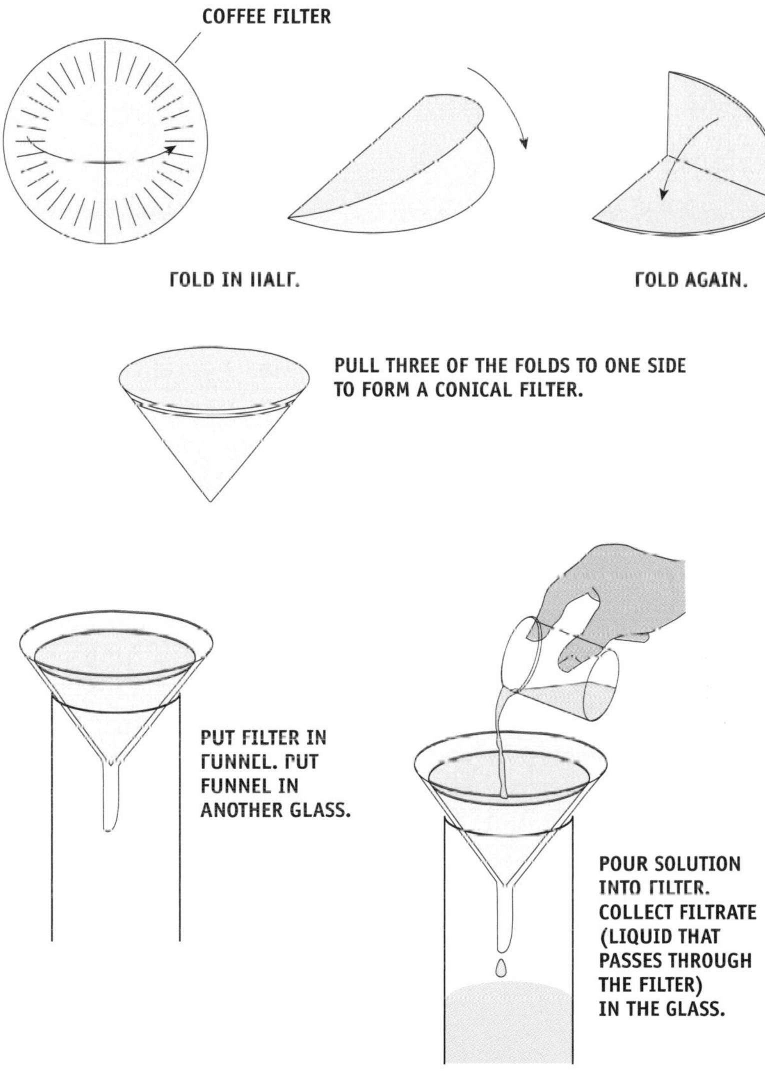

COFFEE FILTER

FOLD IN HALF.

FOLD AGAIN.

PULL THREE OF THE FOLDS TO ONE SIDE TO FORM A CONICAL FILTER.

PUT FILTER IN FUNNEL. PUT FUNNEL IN ANOTHER GLASS.

POUR SOLUTION INTO FILTER. COLLECT FILTRATE (LIQUID THAT PASSES THROUGH THE FILTER) IN THE GLASS.

Making and using a filter to filter a liquid

Remember, do not put any materials in your mouth unless directed to do so.

Can other liquids serve as solvents? Try to dissolve solids that were soluble in water in rubbing alcohol, vinegar, and cooking oil. In which solvents are the solutes soluble? What happens when baking soda is added to vinegar? Can you explain why it happens?

SUBLIMATION

Another way that solids sometimes disappear is sublimation. Solids whose atoms or molecules are not strongly attracted to one another will change from solid to gas without passing through a liquid stage.

If possible, obtain a piece of dry ice. **Ask an adult to help you because dry ice is very cold (–78.5°C or –109°F) and should always be handled while wearing heavy gloves.** Place a small piece of dry ice in a flask or small bottle as you did when you made carbon dioxide in Experiment 4.3. Collect the gas in a balloon as you did in that experiment. Does it weigh more than air?

Iodine crystals will also sublimate. If your school has a fume hood, ask your science teacher to help you gently heat a few iodine crystals in a beaker. **All the apparatus should be in a fume hood that will draw away any vapors so that you do not come in contact with the iodine fumes.** What is the color of gaseous iodine?

Science Fair Project Ideas

- A saturated solution will hold no more solid. Design and carry out experiments to find out how much salt is required to make a saturated solution in 100 ml of room-temperature water. How much sugar is required to make a saturated solution in 100 ml of water?
- Will twice as much solvent dissolve twice as much salt or sugar? Design and carry out experiments to find out.
- Design and carry out experiments to find out whether temperature affects the mass of salt that will dissolve in a fixed volume of water. Does it affect the mass of sugar that will dissolve in a fixed volume of water?
- Investigate the ways in which solubility can be used to help identify solids.
- Investigate the use of iodine vapor in forensic science as a way of making fingerprints visible.
- Investigate solutions made by dissolving gas in liquids. How are these solutions affected by temperature and pressure?

5.2 Making Solids Reappear

Materials:

- salt, sugar, Epsom salts (magnesium sulfate), and alum (potassium aluminum sulfate) (Alum can be obtained at a pharmacy or your school's science lab.)
- measuring teaspoons
- spoons
- metric measuring cup
- water
- glasses
- saucers
- paper and pencil to make labels
- magnifying glass
- hot water

As you saw in the previous experiment, solids disappear when they dissolve in a solvent. They do not reappear if you pour the solution through a filter. Is there any way to make the solids reappear?

One approach might be to let the solution evaporate. Will the solution—both solute and solvent—evaporate, or will the solvent evaporate, leaving the solute behind? To find out, using water as a solvent, prepare separate saturated solutions of salt, sugar, Epsom salts, and alum. A saturated solution is one in which as much solute as possible has dissolved. To prepare a saturated alum solution, add the solute (alum) in level teaspoon quantities to 100 ml of water in a glass. After each teaspoonful, stir with a different spoon until all visible solid has dissolved or until no more will dissolve. Prepare saturated solutions of salt, sugar, and Epsom salts in the same way. Label each solution so that it can be identified. Leave these solutions overnight to be sure that as much solute as possible has dissolved.

On the next day, pour only the solutions into separate saucers, leaving any solid behind. Again place labels beside the saucers so the solutions can be identified. Leave the solutions for several days. Check them periodically.

What do you find happening? Do both solute and solvent evaporate, or does just the solvent evaporate? How can you tell?

Use a magnifying glass to look closely at the substances that remain once the solids are thoroughly dry. You should be able to see small particles with a characteristic shape on each saucer. These particles are crystals. How do the shapes of the crystals on any one saucer compare? How do the shapes of the crystals on different saucers compare?

Which crystals are cubic in shape? Which crystals have a long needle-like shape? Which crystals have hexagonal-shaped faces?

Do you like rock candy? You can make some quite easily. Add 1 cup of sugar to 1/2 cup of hot water. Stir and let stand for a few days. This is one experiment you *can* eat.

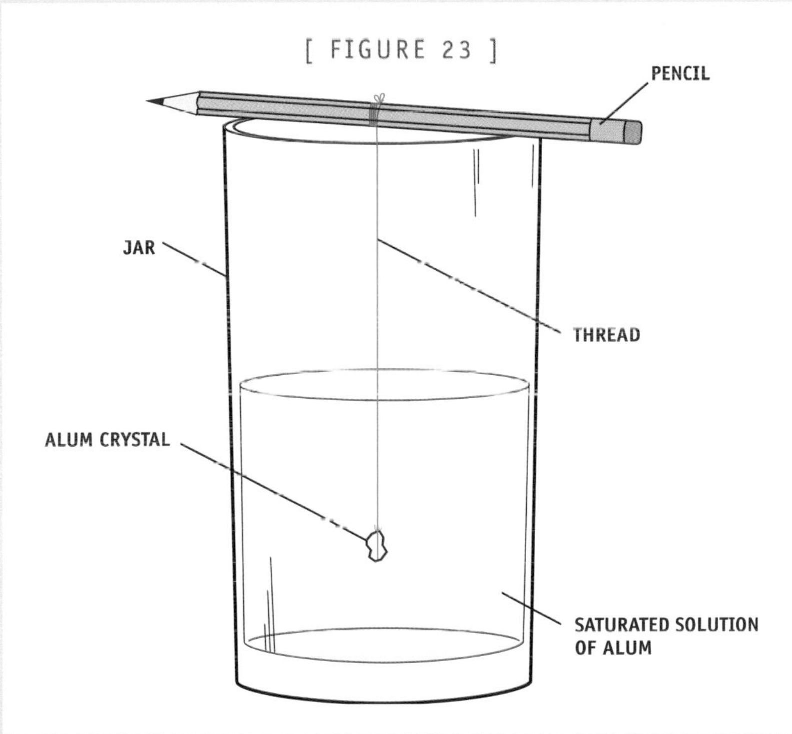

An experiment for growing a large alum crystal

 Science Fair Project Ideas

- Why do you think you were asked to pour the solutions onto saucers? To check on your explanation, pour 100 ml of water into a glass. Pour another 100 ml of water onto a saucer. Leave both in a warm place. Wait and watch for several days. What do you conclude?
- With patience, you can prepare beautiful, large crystals of alum. Prepare a saturated alum solution as before and let it stand overnight to be sure it is saturated. Pour some or all of the solution into a widemouthed jar. Using forceps, pick up one of the crystals from the saucer of alum crystals you prepared. Have someone hold the crystal with the forceps while you attach it to a thread using a slip knot. This will take patience because the crystal is small and delicate. Once you have the crystal on a thread, tie the other end of the thread to a pencil. Lay the pencil across the top of the jar so that the crystal is submerged in the saturated alum solution, as shown in Figure 23. The crystal will grow slowly. If the crystal dissolves, you will know that the solution was not saturated.
- If you succeed in growing a large crystal of alum, you may want to grow your own collection of "gems." Find some books on crystal growing and grow crystals patiently in your "gem garden."

5.3 Making a Liquid Reappear (and a Gas Appear)

Materials:
- an adult
- safety glasses
- teakettle
- water
- stove
- heavy gloves
- drinking glass
- cold water
- ice
- shiny metal can

There is a very simple way to make a liquid reappear and a gas appear. It involves boiling the water and then condensing it.

A liquid's boiling point is the temperature at which it changes to a gas. The bubbles of gas that form in the heated liquid no longer collapse. They rise to the surface and escape.

The change of a gas to a liquid is called condensation. The condensation point of a gaseous substance is the same temperature as the substance's boiling point. If heat is being added, it boils. If heat is being removed, it condenses.

To make a liquid reappear and a gas appear, place a teakettle containing water on a stove. **Put on your safety glasses. Under adult supervision**, turn on the burner. When the water boils, you will see steam coming from the spout of the teakettle. Actually, what most people call steam is really gaseous water that has condensed to tiny droplets of liquid water. If you look closely, you will see a clear region just above the spout. That is where the gaseous water is found.

To change the invisible gas above the spout into liquid water, first **put on a pair of heavy gloves.** Then, **under adult supervision**, hold the bottom of a cold glass of water in the clear gas at the mouth of the teakettle's spout. What do you find collecting and falling from the bottom of the glass? What liquid reappeared? What gas was changed so that it became visible as a liquid?

During warm seasons, especially in the summer, you can make liquids appear just as dew appears on grass after a clear summer night. Do this on a humid day. Fill a shiny metal can with ice. Add water and watch the surface of the can. If the humidity is high, droplets of water will begin to appear on the can's surface. Where do you think they came from? What is humidity?

Science Fair Project Ideas

- One possible explanation for the formation of water droplets on the surface of a can of cold water is that water is leaking through the can. Design an experiment to discover whether water is leaking through the can.
- Investigate the meaning of *dew point*. Then design an experiment to measure the dew point in the room where you found water appearing on the surface of the shiny can of cold water.

5.4 Temperature and Making Liquids Disappear

Materials:
- an adult
- safety glasses
- stove
- small cooking pan
- cold water
- laboratory thermometer with a scale from −10°C to 110°C (You may be able to borrow one from your school's science department.)
- pen or pencil
- notebook
- stopwatch or clock or watch with a second hand
- graph paper

Because you will be using a stove and hot materials in this experiment, you should work under the supervision of an adult. You should also wear safety glasses throughout the experiment.

Turn on one of the small heating elements on a stove. Add cold water to a cooking pan until it is half full. Place a laboratory thermometer that has a scale from −10°C to 110°C in the pan, as shown in Figure 24.

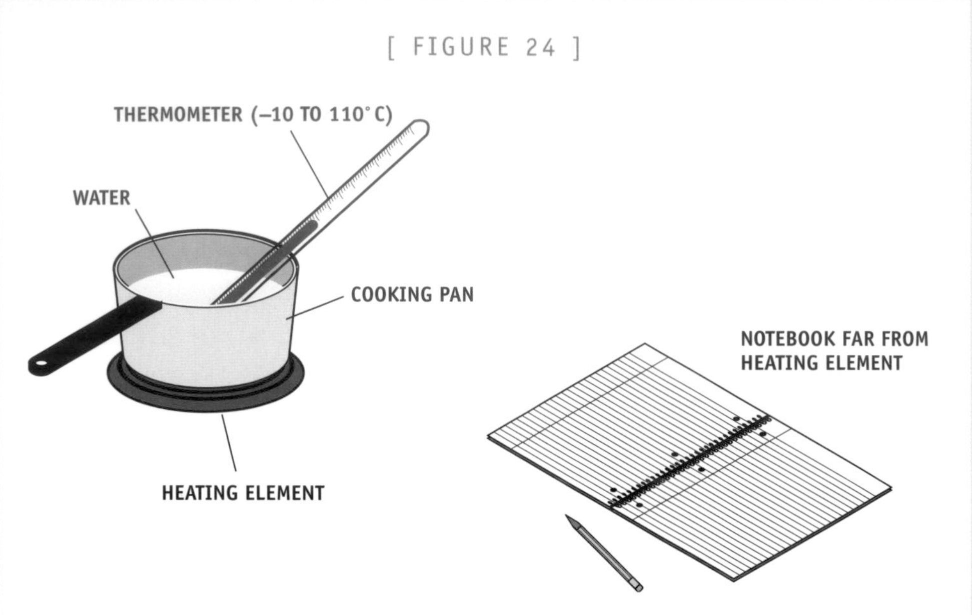

Measuring the temperature of water as it is heated

What is the temperature of the cold water? Next, put the pan of water with the thermometer in it on the stove's heating element.

As the water is being heated, record the water temperature every 1 minute. Use your stopwatch to measure exact 1-minute intervals. Also watch what happens in the water. You will see small bubbles form and rise to the surface. Some of these bubbles are due to air that was dissolved in the water. You may have noticed similar bubbles that form when a cold glass of water is left out overnight. Some of the bubbles result from liquid water changing to gas. When the water begins to boil, the bubbles of water vapor rise vigorously to the surface and burst. What do you notice about the temperature of the water when it begins to boil vigorously?

Continue heating the water until about half of it has changed to a gas. Continue to record the water temperature during this time. What is the temperature? Does it change?

Plot a graph of your data. Make temperature the vertical (*y*) axis of your graph and time the horizontal (*x*) axis. How can you explain the shape of the graph you have plotted?

A TEST OF ANOTHER SUBSTANCE
(Do not try this experiment.)

Using precautions to avoid its flammability, the author heated a small volume of ethyl alcohol to boiling, recorded its temperature over a period of time, and plotted a graph of the data. The graph is shown in Figure 25. What do you conclude about the temperature at which ethyl alcohol boils?

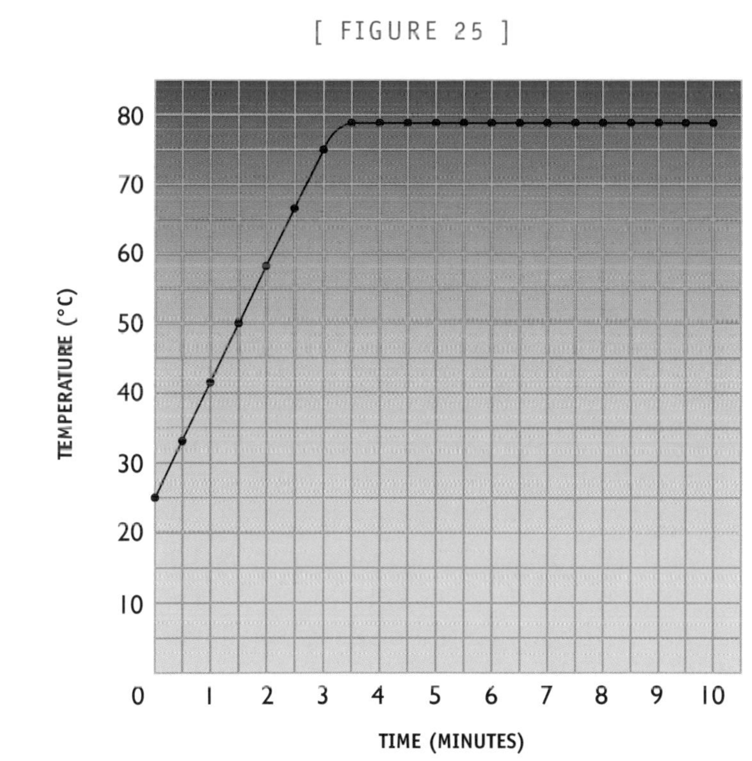

A temperature vs. time graph shows what happens to a small sample of ethyl alcohol when it is heated.

5.5 Making Solids Disappear

Materials:
- chopped ice or snow
- large Styrofoam cup (12 oz)
- thermometer with scale that extends to 0°C (32°F) and below
- plastic pail
- water
- small Styrofoam cup (7 oz)
- scissors
- pen or pencil
- notebook
- freezer
- clock or watch
- graph paper

Put a handful of chopped ice or snow in a large Styrofoam cup. Use a thermometer that can measure temperatures down to and below 0°C (32°F) to stir the ice or snow. What is the lowest temperature the ice or snow reaches as you stir it? Continue stirring the cold solid for several minutes. Does the temperature change or does it remain about the same? At what temperature does ice or snow begin to melt according to your thermometer?

Repeat the experiment with a plastic pail half-filled with chopped ice or snow. Does the mass of the ice or snow affect the temperature at which it melts?

Pour about 50 ml of water into a small Styrofoam cup. Place a thermometer that can measure temperatures down to and below 0°C (32°F) in the water. If necessary, use scissors to cut away part of the side of the cup so that you can see the thermometer scale clearly.

Record the temperature of the water in your notebook. Then put the cup with the water and thermometer in a freezer where you can read the thermometer by simply opening the freezer door. Continue to record the temperature of the water every 10 minutes until the temperature reaches its lowest point. What happens to the temperature while the water is freezing? What happens to the temperature after the water is frozen? Why does the temperature finally reach a minimum?

Leave the frozen water and thermometer in the freezer overnight. On the next day, remove the frozen water from the freezer. Record its temperature at 10-minute intervals until it reaches room temperature.

Using the data you have collected, plot graphs of temperature versus time for the water as it cooled and froze and for the ice as it melted and warmed. You can plot both graphs on the same set of axes.

How does the graph of the water cooling and solidifying compare with the graph of the ice melting and warming to room temperature?

BOILING, FREEZING, MELTING, AND CONDENSING POINTS (TEMPERATURES)

Substances boil or condense at different temperatures; they also melt or freeze at different temperatures. The temperature at which a substance boils (its boiling point) is a characteristic property. Boiling points and melting points are often used to help identify an unknown substance. The boiling, melting, freezing, and condensing points of a few common substances are shown in Table 2. How do the freezing and melting points compare? How do the boiling and condensing points compare?

Which of the substances listed in Table 2 would be liquids at room temperature (around 25°C or 77°F)? Which would be gases? Which would be solids?

TABLE 2

Boiling, condensing, melting, and freezing points of some common substances

Substance	*Boiling point (°C)*	*Condensing point (°C)*	*Melting point (°C)*	*Freezing point (°C)*
Aluminum	**2,519**	**1,800**	**658**	**658**
Lead	**1,749**	**1,525**	**327**	**327**
Salt	**1,465**	**1,413**	**801**	**801**
Mercury	**357**	**357**	**−39**	**−39**
Naphthalene	**218**	**218**	**80**	**80**
Water	**100**	**100**	**0**	**0**
Ethyl alcohol	**78**	**78**	**−117**	**−117**
Methyl alcohol	**65**	**65**	**−98**	**−98**
Oxygen	**−184**	**−184**	**−219**	**−219**
Nitrogen	**−195**	**−195**	**−210**	**−210**
Hydrogen	**−253**	**− 253**	**−259**	**−259**
Helium	**−268**	**−268**	**−271**	**−271**

Science Fair Project Idea

Under adult supervision, place a test tube that is nearly filled with acetamide crystals in a beaker of hot water. (You can probably obtain acetamide from your science teacher or a science supply company through your school.) Heat the water to about 90°C and keep the temperature at that level until all the acetamide melts. Use a test tube clamp to remove the test tube with the melted acetamide from the hot water. Fasten the test tube containing the acetamide to a ring stand. Hang a thermometer from the same ring stand so that its bulb is near the center of the liquid acetamide.

Record the temperature at 30-second intervals until the acetamide crystals reach a temperature close to that of the room. What do you find the freezing temperature of acetamide to be? What would you expect its melting temperature to be? Design and, **under adult supervision**, carry out an experiment to find the melting temperature of acetamide.

5.6 Making a Liquid Appear

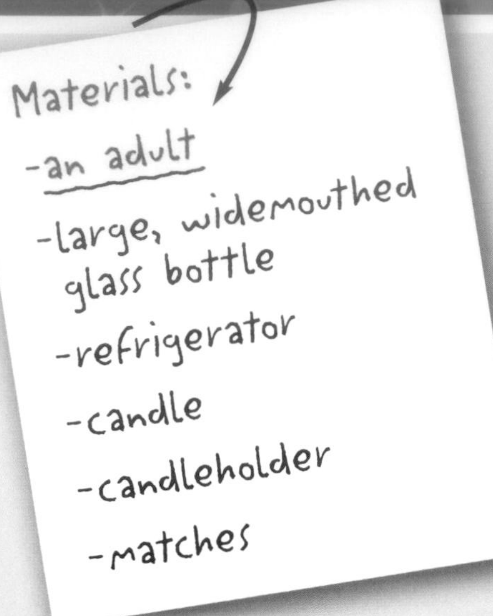

Because you will be using matches and a flame, this experiment should be done under adult supervision.

Chill a large, widemouthed glass bottle in the refrigerator for about 10 minutes. Place a candle in a candleholder and light the candle. When the candle is burning well, hold the cold bottle above the flame, as shown in Figure 26. After several minutes, you should begin to see a thin film of liquid collecting on the sides of the jar. The liquid is water. It is one of the products produced when candle wax burns. The other product (unseen) is carbon dioxide.

[FIGURE 26]

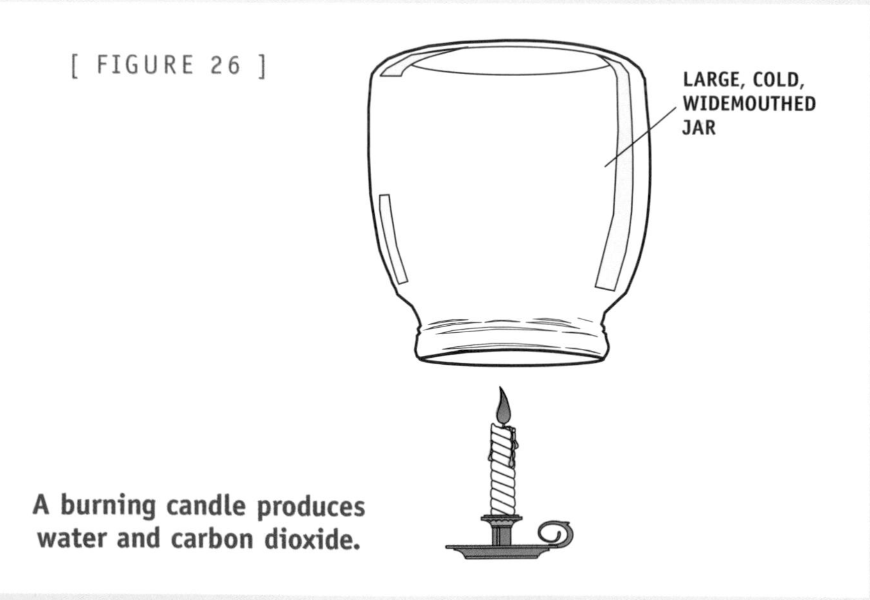

A burning candle produces water and carbon dioxide.

The reaction is summarized by the chemical equation:

candle wax + oxygen → water + carbon dioxide, or
candle wax + O_2 → H_2O + CO_2

The reaction is a chemical change because new substances are formed. You started with candle wax and the oxygen (O_2) in air. These two chemicals combined to form water (H_2O) and carbon dioxide (CO_2). Because the temperature was above water's boiling point, water was produced in the gaseous state. When the gas struck the cold glass, it condensed to liquid water. Based on the fact that water and carbon dioxide were produced when candle wax combined chemically with oxygen, what elements must be present in candle wax?

Science Fair Project Ideas

- Explain why water was evident as a product of this reaction but carbon dioxide was not.
- Investigate how water and carbon dioxide can be identified. Then design and, **under adult supervision**, carry out an experiment to show that the gases produced when a candle burns really are water and carbon dioxide.

5.7 Observing Diffusion of

Materials:

- science teacher
- food coloring
- drinking glasses
- cold water
- hot water
- hydrated copper sulfate ($CuSO_4 \cdot H_2O$)
- small beaker or measuring cup
- graduated cylinder or metric measuring cup
- distilled water
- test tube
- support to keep test tube upright
- eyedropper
- rubber or plastic tubing
- small funnel
- a friend
- bottle of perfume or household ammonia
- ruler
- rubber gloves
- ammonium hydroxide (NH_4OH)
- concentrated hydrochloric acid (HCL)
- watch or clock
- pen or pencil
- notebook
- tape measure

Liquids and Gases

If molecules are in constant motion, you would expect them to spread out, to move through space. The spreading out of molecules through space because they move is called *diffusion*. Of course, the atoms or molecules in solids can only vibrate in place; they are not free to move about one another the way liquid molecules do. In general, therefore, solids do not diffuse. Layers of rocks that have been in contact for millions of years still reveal sharp boundaries. Nevertheless, because of holes (vacancies) in crystals, some solids do diffuse very slowly into other solids.

DIFFUSION OF LIQUIDS

You might expect liquids to diffuse more rapidly because their molecules are free to move about one another. To see if you can observe diffusion in liquids, add a drop of food coloring to a glass of cold water. Watch the colored drop closely. What happens? Can you detect evidence of diffusion?

Based on the molecular model of matter you read about in Chapter 1, how would you expect the rate of diffusion to be affected by temperature?

To test your prediction, place a glass of hot water and a glass of cold water side by side. Be sure there are no gas bubbles or currents in the water. Then add a drop of food coloring to each liquid. Can you see any difference in the rate at which the food coloring diffuses through the water? How long does it take before the color is uniformly spread in each glass? Does temperature affect the rate of diffusion?

The density of food coloring is very close to the density of water. What will happen if you place a denser liquid beneath a less dense one? Will diffusion still occur? Or can gravity overcome upward molecular motion?

To find out, add 4 grams of hydrated copper sulfate ($CuSO_4 \cdot H_2O$) to a small beaker or measuring cup. (You may be able to borrow some copper sulfate from your science teacher.) Add 15 ml of distilled water and stir until all the blue crystals dissolve. Next, add distilled water to a test tube until it is about half full. Support the test tube in an upright position in a place where it will not be disturbed.

To place the blue copper sulfate solution beneath the water in the test tube, you will need an eyedropper (but not the rubber bulb), a length of rubber or plastic tubing, and a small funnel. Attach one end of the tubing to the wide end of the eyedropper and the other end to the funnel, as shown in Figure 27a. Put the end of the eyedropper on the bottom of the test tube. Hold the funnel with one hand and keep the thumb and index finger of your other hand on the tubing so that you can control the flow of liquid through it. Ask a friend to pour the blue solution into the funnel. Then let the solution flow very slowly onto the bottom of the tube beneath the clear water.

After all the liquid has reached the test tube, you will have a blue layer of liquid beneath a clear layer, as seen in Figure 27b. Why does the blue layer of copper sulfate remain under the clear layer of water?

Watch the layers in the tube over the next several weeks. Do you see any evidence of diffusion? If you do, how long does it take before the tube has a uniform color?

DIFFUSION OF GASES

You might expect gases to diffuse more rapidly than liquids because their molecules are farther apart. On the other hand, there are fewer of them in a given volume and, if released into air, they will bump into air molecules as they move.

One way to look for the diffusion of gases is to have a partner open a bottle of perfume or household ammonia. Stand several meters from the bottle, record the time, and wait. How long does it take before your sense of smell tells you that the gas molecules of perfume or ammonia have reached you?

Measure the distance between you and the bottle. Use the distance and time to determine the average speed of the molecules. These molecules are actually moving at more than 100 meters per second. Why did it take so long for them to travel the short distance between you and the bottle from which they came?

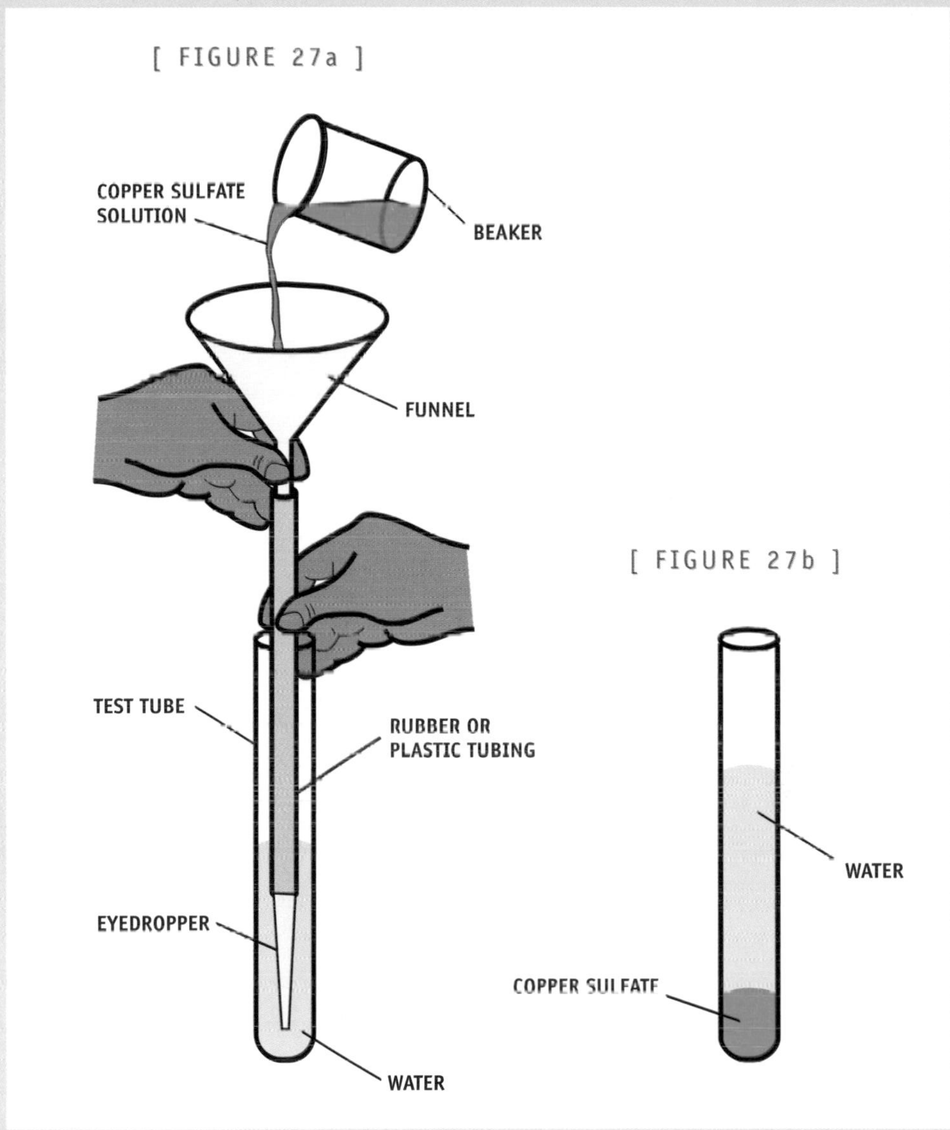

27a) The diagram shows how a layer of copper sulfate can be placed under a layer of water. b) Two distinct layers are shown in a test tube.

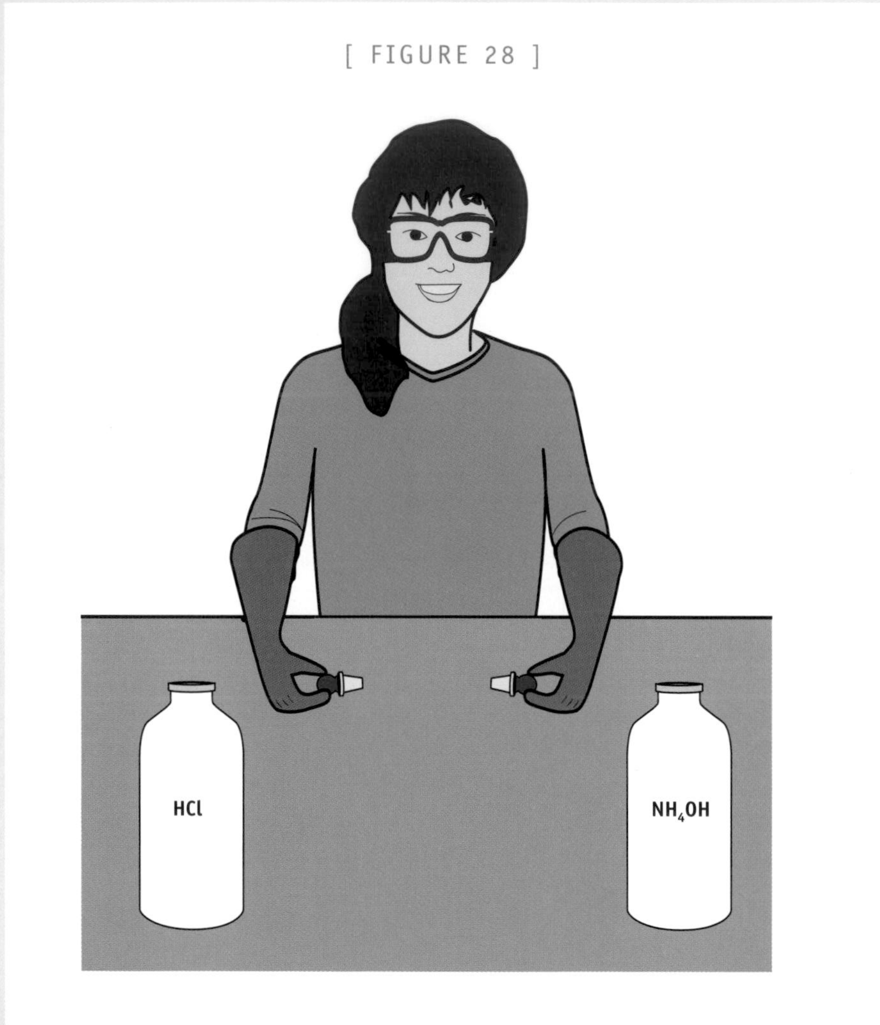

An experiment to see if hydrogen chloride and ammonia will diffuse and form a white cloud of ammonium chloride

Ask your science teacher to help you with another experiment to show that gases diffuse. Place a bottle of ammonium hydroxide (NH_4OH) about 1 meter away from a bottle of concentrated hydrochloric acid (HCl). Wearing rubber gloves, use one hand to remove the glass stopper from the bottle of hydrochloric acid. With your other hand, remove the stopper from the bottle that holds ammonium hydroxide. Keeping the two stoppers about half a meter apart, give the gaseous fumes from the two solutions time to diffuse (see Figure 28). If they diffuse far enough from the stoppers to meet, you will see a white cloud form. The cloud is ammonium chloride, a white solid that forms when hydrogen chloride (HCl) gas, which comes from the hydrochloric acid, and ammonia (NH_3) gas, which comes from the ammonium hydroxide, combine. The formula for the reaction is

$$HCl + NH_3 \longrightarrow NH_4Cl$$

Does a white cloud form? How were the reactants (HCl and NH_3), which were half a meter apart, able to combine to form the product (NH_4Cl)?

Science Fair Project Idea

Design an experiment that will allow you to estimate the relative molecular speeds of ammonia and hydrogen chloride. **With the help of your science teacher,** carry out the experiment. What do you find their relative molecular speeds to be?

5.8 How Does Sugar Affect

Materials:
- measuring cup
- 3 clear, disposable plastic cups
- water
- cola (not diet)
- corn syrup
- freezer
- watch or clock

In this experiment you will try to determine if cola has a lower freezing point than water. In addition, you will determine how the amount of sugar in cola compares to pure water and to corn syrup and how this affects freezing point.

Pour 1/2 cup of water into a clear plastic cup. Place 1/2 cup of cola (not diet) into a second plastic cup. Add 1/2 cup of corn syrup to a third cup. Place the three cups in a freezer (see Figure 29).

Check the cups each hour for 5 hours and then check after they have been in the freezer for a total of at least 24 hours. When you check a cup, tilt it to the side and observe if there is liquid, solid, or both present. Corn syrup is a viscous (slow-flowing) liquid, so you may have to wait 10 to 30 seconds to see if it is flowing when you tilt the corn syrup cup. When you check the cups, also touch the top of the water, cola, and syrup to see how each one feels. As soon as you are finished observing each cup, immediately return it to the freezer. In your science notebook, record the total time in the freezer and your observations for each liquid.

The temperature of freezers varies somewhat, but freezers are always set below the freezing point of water. Water freezes at 0°C (32°F). A typical temperature for a freezer is about –7°C (20°F). At this low temperature, would you expect water to change from a liquid to a solid? How long did it take for the water to freeze? Water freezes at the top first, and then the rest of the water freezes into one solid piece.

Did the corn syrup remain a liquid even after 24 hours in the freezer? Corn syrup is thick and viscous because it has many sugar molecules dissolved in water. The sugar molecules cause the water to have a lower

Place cups with water, cola, and corn syrup in a freezer. Check the cups after 1, 2, 3, 4, 5, and 24 hours to see if the liquids have frozen solid.

freezing point. Molecules added to water make it more difficult for the water molecules to form a solid. If the corn syrup has a freezing point below the temperature of your freezer, then it will remain a liquid.

Colas are usually sweetened with either fructose sugar molecules made from corn syrup or sucrose sugar molecules. Which would you expect to have a lower freezing point—water or cola? Which took longer to freeze in your experiment—water, cola, or corn syrup? Did the cola freeze? Did the corn syrup freeze? Do you think cola or corn syrup has more sugar molecules?

Science Fair Project Idea

Repeat this experiment using cups containing pure water, water with known amounts of sugar, regular soft drinks, and diet soft drinks. Use several different types of soft drinks. Record your observations about how long it takes the liquids to freeze to a solid and how they look. Do the diet drinks behave more like the water or more like the sugar-containing soft drinks? Can you explain why?

5.9 How Does Salt Affect Carbonated Beverages?

Materials:
- unopened bottle of cola
- bowl
- stopwatch or clock or watch with a second hand
- salt shaker

In this experiment you will find out if salt and other solids can be used to test for the presence of dissolved carbon dioxide.

Open a bottle of cola and gently pour some into a bowl to a depth of about 1 inch. Wait about 30 seconds until any foam has cleared from the top of the liquid. Sprinkle salt from a salt shaker on top of the liquid in the bowl. What happens? Do you hear fizzing and see bubbles forming?

Wait about 30 seconds more and then sprinkle salt on the cola again. Repeat this activity as many times as you choose. Are bubbles formed every time? How many times can you sprinkle salt and see a cloud of bubbles form?

Carbonated drinks have carbon dioxide gas dissolved in the liquid. This carbon dioxide will slowly come out of the soda if it is left open to the air. You can test any carbonated soda to see if it still has dissolved gas in it or if it has lost its dissolved carbon dioxide and gone flat. Sprinkle salt in a small sample of the soda you wish to test and observe if any bubbles form.

When pure water or a sugar water mixture boils, water molecules leave the liquid and go into the gas phase. The molecules move faster and farther apart as they leave the surface of the liquid and spread into the room air. The bubbles that are seen in boiling water are small pockets of hot, gaseous water rising to the surface of the liquid. Hot liquids including water can boil up suddenly if small amounts of solid particles are added. **Caution: Do not sprinkle salt or solid particles on a hot liquid.**

In this experiment, the small particles of salt provide surfaces where gas can collect and larger bubbles can form. This process of providing sites for other gases or molecules to collect is called *nucleation*. Carbon dioxide molecules gather on the surface of the salt and form larger bubbles of gas that rise to the top of the liquid.

Nucleation is sometimes used to try to make it rain in a process called cloud seeding. There are several different methods of seeding clouds. In one method, a plane is used to drop small particles of silver iodide into a cloud where the temperature is below 0°C (32°F). The cold water vapor in the cloud forms ice crystals on the solid particles, and the ice crystals fall to the ground. On the way to the ground, the ice crystals melt and become rain. Cloud seeding does not always work, and some states prohibit it because of fears that it may disrupt natural patterns of rainfall.

Science Fair Project Ideas

- Repeat the activity above while adding the same amounts of different types of solids such as salt, sugar, baking soda, sand, and pepper. Try different clear carbonated drinks such as Mountain Dew, Sprite, Mello Yello, or 7UP. Make a chart of your results trying different solids and different drinks. Which drinks give the most fizz? Which solids cause the most bubbles to be released?
- Allow different sodas to remain open to the air and test them for fizz several times each day for four days. Make a chart of your results and compare how long it takes for different sodas to lose all their fizz.

5.10 How Does Phosphoric Acid Affect Metal Oxides?

Materials:
- 3 older brown pennies (made before 1983)
- bowl
- cola that contains phosphoric acid
- new shiny penny
- paper towel

When a penny is new, it has a shiny copper surface. Pennies minted since 1983 are made of zinc and covered with a thin layer of copper. Over time the penny's copper surface changes to a dull brown. This change in color is due to a layer of copper oxide that forms on the surface. Oxygen from the air combines with copper to make the brown copper oxide. In this experiment, you will find out if you can use cola that contains phosphoric acid in a chemical reaction to remove the copper oxide layer.

Place two older brown pennies—head side up—in a bowl. Cover the pennies with cola about 2.5 cm (1 in) deep. After about 30 minutes turn the pennies over to place them tail side up in the bowl. After another 30 minutes remove the pennies and pour out the cola from the bowl. Be sure to thoroughly clean the bowl at the end of your experiment. Observe the pennies and compare them to the third old brown penny that was not cleaned. Wipe the pennies with a paper towel to dry them. Do the old, cleaned pennies look more like the remaining old one or the new shiny penny?

The cola contains phosphoric acid (H_3PO_4). When copper oxide (CuO) is placed in an acid, copper ions (Cu^{2+}) are released and water (H_2O) molecules are formed. The copper oxide layer on an old penny dissolves in acid. As the copper oxide layer is removed, it reveals a clean copper surface underneath.

Science Fair Project Ideas

- Repeat this activity using as many different soft drinks as you can find. Some soft drinks contain phosphoric acid, while others contain citric acid. Some drinks contain both phosphoric and citric acids. Is there any difference in cleaning ability between citric acid and phosphoric acid? Is there any difference between diet and regular drinks in cleaning pennies? Try to rate different sodas by their cleaning ability and compare these results to the contents of the drinks.
- Rust is a combination of iron and oxygen atoms. Test and compare different sodas in their ability to remove rust. Find rusted iron or steel objects such as old nails. Or you can make rusted objects by leaving wet iron nails exposed to the air for several days. Place these rusted objects in jars and cover with different sodas. Leave for an hour, then remove the objects and dry with a paper towel. Was the rust removed? Try to rate different sodas for their cleaning ability and compare these results to the contents of the drinks.

FURTHER READING

Books

Baldwin, Carol. ***States of Matter.*** Chicago: Raintree, 2004.

Bochinski, Julianne Blair. ***The Complete Workbook for Science Fair Projects.*** Hoboken, N.J.: John Wiley and Sons, Inc., 2005.

Encyclopedia of Earth and Physical Sciences. New York: Marshall Cavendish, 2005.

Levine, Shar, and Leslie Johnstone. ***Kitchen Science.*** New York: Sterling Publishing Co., 2003.

Moorman, Thomas. ***How to Make Your Science Project Scientific.*** Revised Edition. New York: John Wiley & Sons, Inc., 2002.

Newcomb, Rain, and Bobby Mercer. ***Smash It! Crash It! Launch It! 50 Mind-Blowing, Eye-Popping Science Experiments.*** New York: Lark Books, 2006.

Internet Addresses

Society for Science and the Public. *Science News for Kids.* 2008.
<http://www.sciencenewsforkids.org/>

Funburst Media LLC. *Funology: The Science of Having Fun.* 2008.
<http://www.funology.com/>

Try Science/New York Hall of Science. *Try Science . . . home.* 1999–2008.
<http://tryscience.org/experiments/experiments_home.html>

INDEX

W